BREAKING FREE FROM ANXIETY:
PROVEN TECHNIQUES TO REGAIN CONTROL OF YOUR LIFE

Introduction

In the whirlwind of today's world, anxiety has quietly become a significant force, touching our lives in subtle yet profound ways. If you've ever felt the weight of worry or the uneasy dance of unease, know that you're not on this journey alone. As someone deeply connected to mental health, I warmly invite you to join me on a journey through the pages of "Breaking Free from Anxiety: Proven Techniques to Regain Control of Your Life."

This book transcends mere words; it's your compassionate companion, a guiding light that intimately understands and acknowledges the challenges brought by anxiety. Envision it as a supportive friend on your journey, providing comfort and illuminating the path toward a life brimming with peace and control. Beyond sharing information, my purpose is to be a wellspring of hope.

Let's acknowledge anxiety—a common thread in our lives. Through stories and facts, we'll shine a light on its impact and lay the groundwork for practical tools that lie ahead.

As we turn the pages, we'll unravel the mystery of anxiety together, exploring its roots without complex jargon. This isn't just about understanding; it's about creating a foundation where simple practices like breathing become tools for change. Expect insights to lift your spirits and discussions about the power of a strong support system—an essential lifeline towards a future free from anxiety.

Are you ready to break free? Let's embark on this journey together, transcending anxiety and discovering a life filled with lasting well-being and personal growth.

Chapter 1: Understanding Anxiety

Uncover the interplay of biological and psychological mechanisms contributing to anxiety, exploring various anxiety disorders and revealing compelling statistics. Comprehensive lists and self-assessment tools aid in recognizing anxiety symptoms. Identify triggers, track patterns, and engage in self-reflection using provided journal prompts. Explore the mind-body connection, understanding how anxiety impacts physical health and vice versa, with inspiring stories of holistic approaches. Demystify anxiety through evidence-based information, debunking common myths to offer reassurance and instill hope.

The Intricate Symphony of Anxiety

At its core, anxiety unfolds like a symphony—a dynamic interplay orchestrated by the delicate dance of both biology and psychology. Picture the brain as a maestro skillfully conducting the intricate harmony of neurotransmitters, hormones, and cognitive processes. This symphony isn't confined to the present moment; it resonates through the corridors of our genetic heritage, weaving a narrative beyond the boundaries of time.

A Maestro's Touch: The Brain's Orchestration

Our journey commences in the emotional processing center—the amygdala—a maestro in the symphony of anxiety orchestrating responses to perceived threats. This key player sets the stage for emotional crescendos, while the prefrontal cortex, our seat of rationality, enters the composition, attempting to bring order to these emotional peaks. Exploring these biological nuances unveils the realization that anxiety is not a mere emotional state but a symphony of neural activities intricately shaping our perception of the world.

Neurotransmitters and Hormones: Messengers of Emotion

To truly understand anxiety's essence, we delve into the intricate dance of neurotransmitters and hormones within the brain. Visualize neurotransmitters as messengers conveying vital information between nerve cells. In the symphony of anxiety, these messengers play a crucial role, influencing how our brain processes emotions and reacts to stimuli.

Consider serotonin, the "feel-good" neurotransmitter, contributing to mood regulation. Imbalances can lead to heightened anxiety. Similarly, norepinephrine, associated with the body's fight-or-flight response, surges during anxious moments, preparing us for potential threats. This understanding of neurotransmitters provides insight into the chemical intricacies that contribute to the symphony of anxiety.

Hormones, the body's chemical messengers, join this dance, amplifying emotional notes. Cortisol, released in response to stress, plays a pivotal role. During anxious episodes, cortisol levels spike, affecting various bodily functions. This hormonal interplay intertwines with neural activities, shaping the rhythm and intensity of our anxious experiences.

The Cognitive Ballet: Thinking Patterns

Beyond neurotransmitters and hormones, the cognitive processes within the brain form a crucial part of anxiety's symphony. Our thoughts and interpretations of events contribute to the emotional crescendos orchestrated by anxiety. The amygdala collaborates with cognitive regions to craft our perception of threats and challenges.

Cognitive distortions, like catastrophizing or overgeneralization, become integral notes in this symphony. These thinking patterns, often automatic and unconscious, influence how we interpret situations, fueling anxiety. By unraveling these cognitive intricacies, we gain insight into the mental aspects of anxiety—not only understanding what happens within the brain but how our thoughts contribute to the symphonic composition.

The Genetic Prelude: Nature and Nurture

Anxiety's symphony is a continuous journey, weaving echoes from our genetic heritage. Genetic predispositions contribute to the orchestration of anxiety, influencing how our brain responds to environmental stressors. Exploring this genetic component helps us recognize that anxiety is a multifaceted symphony, woven from the threads of both nature and nurture.

As our understanding deepens, it becomes clear that this symphony is dynamic and ever-changing. By peeling back the layers and exploring the intricate choreography of neurotransmitters, hormones, cognitive processes, and genetic predispositions, we embark on a journey toward a comprehensive comprehension of anxiety—an understanding that transcends the surface and delves into the symphonic depths of our being.

Diverse Movements in the Symphony: Exploring Anxiety Disorders

As we delve further into the intricate symphony of anxiety, it's crucial to acknowledge that this emotional composition takes on various forms, each presenting unique movements and expressions. Just as different instruments contribute to the richness of a symphony, various anxiety disorders add complexity to the emotional landscape. Let's immerse ourselves in these diverse movements, gaining an understanding of the nuanced facets of anxiety that weave through the tapestry of human experience.

Generalized Anxiety Disorder (GAD)

Envision a constant hum in the background—an ever-present worry that colors every aspect of life. This defines the essence of Generalized Anxiety Disorder (GAD), a movement in the symphony of anxiety characterized by persistent and excessive worrying about various aspects of daily life. From work to relationships, individuals with GAD often find themselves entangled in the relentless rhythm of apprehension, unable to escape the pervasive unease.

Social Anxiety Disorder

Imagine a delicate dance on the stage of social interactions, where the fear of judgment takes center stage. Social Anxiety Disorder is a movement that manifests as an overwhelming fear of being scrutinized or negatively evaluated in social situations. The anxiety can be so profound that it hinders one's ability to engage in social activities, impacting relationships, work, and overall quality of life.

Panic Disorder

In the symphony of anxiety, sudden and intense crescendos mark the presence of Panic Disorder. Picture an abrupt surge of fear, accompanied by physical symptoms like a racing heart, shortness of breath, and a sense of impending doom. Panic attacks become the focal points of this movement, disrupting the regular flow of life and leaving individuals grappling with the aftermath of these emotional storms.

Obsessive-Compulsive Disorder (OCD)

Enter a meticulous and repetitive sequence of notes—an intricate pattern that demands adherence. Obsessive-Compulsive Disorder (OCD) introduces a unique movement to the symphony of anxiety. Individuals with OCD experience persistent, intrusive thoughts (obsessions) that drive them to perform ritualistic behaviors (compulsions) in an attempt to alleviate the anxiety associated with these thoughts. This constant interplay of thoughts and actions creates a distinctive rhythm within the symphony.

Post-Traumatic Stress Disorder (PTSD)

Imagine echoes of a past trauma reverberating through the symphony—an emotional composition haunted by memories. Post-Traumatic Stress Disorder (PTSD) introduces a poignant movement shaped by exposure to a traumatic event. Flashbacks, nightmares, and severe emotional distress characterize this disorder, highlighting the enduring impact of past experiences on one's emotional landscape.

Specific Phobias

In this movement, individual fears take center stage, dominating the emotional composition. Specific Phobias involve an intense and irrational fear of a particular object, situation, or activity. This fear can be so overwhelming that it leads to avoidance behaviors, shaping the individual's life around steering clear of the perceived threat.

As we explore these diverse movements within the symphony of anxiety, it's crucial to understand that individuals may experience a blend of these disorders, creating a unique composition for each person.

Unveiling the Impact: Surprising Statistics on Anxiety

Now, let's shine a spotlight on some compelling facts and surprising statistics that underscore the prevalence and significance of anxiety in our lives. As we delve into the symphony of anxiety, it's essential to grasp the magnitude of its influence on the human experience.

Global Reach of Anxiety

Anxiety is not confined to specific regions—it's a global phenomenon. According to the World Health Organization (WHO), an estimated 264 million people worldwide grapple with anxiety disorders, making it one of the most prevalent mental health issues globally.

Rising Trends Among Youth

The symphony of anxiety often finds a prominent audience among the youth. Recent studies indicate a concerning rise in anxiety disorders among adolescents and young adults. The pressure of modern life, academic challenges, and social dynamics contribute to this upward trend.

Gender Dynamics

The symphony resonates differently across genders. Women are statistically more likely to experience anxiety disorders than men. This gender difference in prevalence suggests a nuanced interplay of biological, psychological, and societal factors.

The Economic Impact

Anxiety not only affects individuals but also reverberates through economies. The economic burden of anxiety disorders is substantial, with costs associated with healthcare, productivity loss, and disability accommodations. It's a reminder that the symphony of anxiety extends beyond personal experiences.

Comorbidity with Other Conditions

Anxiety often shares the stage with other mental health conditions. Studies reveal a high prevalence of comorbidity, where individuals with anxiety disorders may also experience depression, substance abuse, or other psychiatric challenges. This interplay adds layers to the symphony, influencing its complexity.

Impact on Physical Health

The symphony of anxiety echoes in both the mind and body. Research highlights the intricate connection between anxiety and physical health. Individuals with anxiety disorders may be at a higher risk of various health issues, emphasizing the importance of addressing anxiety comprehensively.

Treatment Disparities

Despite the prevalence of anxiety, there are notable disparities in seeking and receiving treatment. Many individuals, for various reasons, do not access the support they need. This gap in treatment underscores the importance of fostering awareness and reducing stigmas surrounding mental health.

Embrace Your Influence:

Anxiety's impact extends beyond moments of distress. It influences daily functioning, affecting work, relationships, and overall quality of life. Understanding the pervasive nature of anxiety emphasizes the need for comprehensive strategies and support systems.

These facts and statistics provide a glimpse into the vast landscape of anxiety. As we navigate the symphony, it's crucial to recognize that the melodies are not isolated notes but interconnected threads woven into the fabric of our shared human experience. By acknowledging the prevalence and impact of anxiety, we take a collective step toward fostering understanding, compassion, and effective strategies for managing this intricate composition.

Recognizing Anxiety Symptoms

Understanding anxiety requires the recognition and comprehension of its symptoms, which are pivotal for effective self-management. Anxiety is a multifaceted experience that reverberates through the mind and body, influencing physical, emotional, and behavioral realms. Navigating these symptoms with awareness and understanding is essential to foster effective coping mechanisms and self-care strategies.

Physical Symptoms:

- Racing Heart: A palpable heartbeat, often accompanied by a feeling of restlessness.
- Shortness of Breath: Difficulty breathing or a sense of breathlessness.
- Muscle Tension: Tightness or stiffness in muscles, especially in the neck and shoulders.
- Sweating: Unexplained perspiration, even in non-strenuous situations.
- Dizziness: Feeling lightheaded or unsteady.
- Nausea or Upset Stomach: Digestive discomfort or a churning sensation.
- Fatigue: Persistent tiredness or exhaustion.
- Insomnia: Difficulty falling asleep or staying asleep.

Emotional Symptoms:

- Excessive Worrying: Persistent and uncontrollable thoughts of potential negative outcomes.
- Irritability: Easily becoming agitated or on edge.
- Feeling Overwhelmed: A sense of being unable to cope with daily challenges.
- Restlessness: Difficulty staying still or a constant need to move.
- Trouble Concentrating: Difficulty focusing or a racing mind.
- Fear of Losing Control: A pervasive sense of impending doom or loss of control.
- Feeling On Edge: Heightened alertness or sensitivity to surroundings.

Behavioral Symptoms:

- Avoidance: Steering clear of situations or places that trigger anxiety.
- Procrastination: Delaying tasks due to anxiety about potential outcomes.
- Compulsive Behaviors: Repetitive actions performed to alleviate anxiety.
- Isolation: Withdrawing from social activities or interactions.
- Seeking Reassurance: Constantly seeking validation or reassurance from others.
- Changes in Eating Habits: Either increased or decreased appetite.
- Impaired Performance: A decline in work, academic, or social performance.

Tools for Self-Reflection and Insight:

Recognizing anxiety symptoms involves a journey of self-reflection and insight. Here are self-assessment tools designed to aid readers in understanding their anxiety levels:

- Anxiety Symptom Checklist: A comprehensive tool for individuals to mark and reflect on the presence of various anxiety symptoms.
- Daily Mood Journal: Encourages readers to track their daily mood, identifying patterns and correlations with anxiety symptoms.
- Fear Hierarchy: A structured approach for ranking and understanding specific fears or triggers on different levels.
- Stress Diary: Helps individuals pinpoint stressors and assess their impact on anxiety levels.

Narratives That Echo the Symphony of Anxiety:

To humanize the experience of anxiety, let's explore relatable anecdotes that mirror the diverse and complex nature of anxiety:

- Emily's Racing Heart: Emily's poignant narrative articulates the palpitations of her heart during work presentations, revealing the physical manifestation of anxiety.
- Alex's Sleepless Nights: Alex candidly shares his struggles with insomnia, attributing it to persistent worry about future uncertainties and its impact on overall well-being.
- Sophie's Avoidance Patterns: Sophie vulnerably narrates her journey of avoiding social gatherings due to the fear of judgment, shedding light on behavioral symptoms and the impact on social interactions.
- Jake's Compulsive Rituals: Jake openly discusses his daily rituals and compulsions, providing insight into the coping mechanisms individuals adopt to manage anxiety.

Embrace the Signs:

By recognizing the diverse symphony of anxiety symptoms, engaging with self-assessment tools, and connecting with relatable anecdotes, readers embark on a profound journey of self-discovery. This knowledge serves as a compass, guiding individuals towards a deeper understanding of their experiences and fostering compassion and resilience in the face of anxiety's challenges.

Identifying Triggers and Patterns: Decoding the Language of Anxiety

Continuing our exploration of the intricate symphony of anxiety, our focus now shifts to the roots that intricately weave its composition. Understanding the significance of triggers and patterns emerges as a pivotal theme in navigating the multifaceted nature of anxiety. This chapter endeavors to offer practical insights, empowering you, the reader, on your journey toward effective anxiety management.

Triggers serve as catalysts, setting the emotional symphony in motion, while patterns represent the recurring melodies that shape its composition. Identifying and comprehending these elements is akin to deciphering the language of anxiety—a fundamental step in your journey toward self-management.

Practical Insights for Your Journey:

Understanding triggers and patterns isn't a theoretical exercise; it's a practical endeavor with real-life applications. Here's how you can actively engage with this chapter to gain valuable insights into your anxiety:

Initiating Self-Reflection:

Begin by considering instances when anxiety has been particularly pronounced. Explore the circumstances, environments, or thoughts that preceded these moments. The following journal prompts have been thoughtfully crafted to guide this introspective process.

Journal Prompt 1: Reflect on a recent episode of heightened anxiety. What was happening around you, and what thoughts were occupying your mind?

Identifying Triggers:

Triggers are the catalysts that initiate the symphony of anxiety. By identifying these triggers, you can gain control over your emotional responses. Utilize the provided tools, such as the Trigger Tracker, to offer a structured approach to pinpointing these catalysts.

Trigger Tracker: Document situations, events, or thoughts that trigger anxiety. Categorize them based on their nature and intensity.

Tracking Patterns:

Patterns provide insights into the recurring themes within the symphony of anxiety. Through consistent self-monitoring using tools like the Pattern Journal, you can uncover the rhythms and repetitions in your anxious experiences.

Pattern Journal: Regularly record your emotional states, thoughts, and external factors. Identify any recurrent patterns or themes that emerge over time.

Encouraging Your Self-Reflection:

Engaging with the journal prompts fosters a journey of self-discovery. These prompts are not mere exercises but gateways to a deeper understanding of your triggers and patterns. As you embark on this self-reflective process, consider the following:

- What recurrent themes emerge in your anxious moments?
- Are there specific situations or environments consistently linked to heightened anxiety?
- How do your thoughts contribute to the amplification of anxiety, and are there patterns in these cognitive processes?

Embrace the Work:

By actively participating in these self-reflective exercises, you harness the power to unravel the intricate threads of your anxiety. This chapter serves as a guide, equipping you with the tools and insights needed to identify, comprehend, and ultimately manage the triggers and patterns woven into your unique symphony of anxiety.

Nurturing the Mind-Body Connection: Harmony Amidst Turbulence

As we gracefully navigate through the symphony of anxiety, our focus now turns to the intricate interplay between the mind and body—a dynamic relationship that forms the essence of our being. Building upon our exploration of triggers and patterns, this chapter immerses us in the vital realm of the mind-body connection, accentuating the pursuit of harmony amidst the turbulence of anxiety.

Significance of a Healthy Mind-Body Balance:

Promoting a healthy mind-body balance transcends luxury; it stands as a fundamental necessity in the journey of anxiety management. The interconnectedness of mental and physical well-being lays the groundwork for resilience, providing a stable foundation to navigate the ebb and flow of life's challenges.

Practices for Cultivating Equilibrium:

The pursuit of harmony amidst turbulence involves practical and actionable strategies. Let's delve into practices that empower you to foster a robust mind-body connection, promoting resilience in the face of anxiety:

Mindful Breathing Techniques:

Begin your journey by anchoring yourself in the present moment through mindful breathing. The Breath Awareness Exercise, detailed below, serves as a simple yet potent tool to ground your awareness.

Breath Awareness Exercise:

Inhale deeply for a count of four, hold your breath for four counts, exhale for four counts, and pause for another four counts. Repeat this rhythmic cycle, allowing your breath to guide you into a state of calm awareness.

Progressive Muscle Relaxation (PMR):

Recognize and release tension in your body through Progressive Muscle Relaxation. The provided Muscle Relaxation Guide offers a step-by-step approach to systematically relax different muscle groups, promoting physical and mental relaxation.

Muscle Relaxation Guide:

Starting from your toes, tense and then release each muscle group, working your way up to the top of your head. Pay attention to the sensations of tension and release in each area.

Holistic Well-Being Practices:

Explore activities that nurture both your mental and physical health. Engage in regular exercise, maintain a balanced diet, prioritize sufficient sleep, and cultivate mindfulness through practices like meditation or yoga.

Holistic Well-Being Planner:

Use the planner to set achievable goals for maintaining a healthy lifestyle. Track your progress in areas such as exercise, nutrition, sleep, and mindfulness.

Integration of Transformative Stories:

Within these strategies and exercises, narratives of transformation shared by individuals who have navigated their own symphony of anxiety seamlessly weave into the fabric of this chapter. These stories illustrate the transformative power arising from cultivating a harmonious mind-body connection.

Amanda's Journey to Mindful Living:

Amanda, amidst the chaos of urban life, discovered the power of mindful living. Through daily meditation and mindful practices, she not only alleviated anxiety symptoms but also developed a profound connection between her mind and body. Amanda's story illustrates the transformative potential of embracing mindfulness in navigating life's challenges.

Michael's Embrace of Physical Activity:

For Michael, anxiety found an unexpected adversary in the form of physical activity. Engaging in regular exercise became a therapeutic outlet, releasing the grip of anxiety and empowering him with a renewed sense of vitality. Michael's journey highlights the profound impact of incorporating movement into the holistic approach to well-being.

Sara's Nutritional Empowerment:

Sara's journey toward managing anxiety took a nutritional turn. Through informed dietary choices, she discovered the influence of nutrition on mental health. By prioritizing nourishing foods and adopting a mindful approach to eating, Sara found herself on a path of holistic well-being, where the mind and body coexisted harmoniously.

Embrace Intentionality:

In embracing the mind-body connection, you embark on a journey toward resilience—a journey marked by intentional practices, self-discovery, and the realization that the harmonious interplay between mind and body is an instrumental key to managing the symphony of anxiety.

Debunking Myths About Anxiety: Unveiling Truths and Embracing Hope

In the intricate realm of anxiety, myths and misconceptions can cast shadows, perpetuating fears and hindering the journey toward understanding and healing. This chapter serves as a guiding light, dispelling the mist of misinformation and illuminating evidence-based truths that bring reassurance and hope. Let's delve deeper to debunk common myths, replacing uncertainty with clarity and fear with empowerment.

Myth: Anxiety Is Just a Passing Phase

Truth: Anxiety is a valid and persistent emotional experience.

One prevalent myth suggests that anxiety is a transient emotional state that will naturally fade away. In reality, anxiety can be a chronic condition that persists over time, impacting various aspects of an individual's life. By acknowledging its validity, we open the door to understanding and seeking effective strategies for managing anxiety.

Myth: Anxiety Is a Sign of Weakness

Truth: Anxiety is not indicative of personal weakness; it is a complex interplay of biological and environmental factors.

Dispelling the notion that anxiety reflects weakness is essential. Anxiety arises from a complex interplay of genetic predispositions, brain chemistry, and environmental factors. Understanding these multifaceted origins helps dismantle the stigma associated with anxiety, fostering compassion and empathy.

Myth: Anxiety Is a Choice

Truth: Anxiety is not a choice but a complex interplay of biological and environmental factors.

Contrary to the belief that individuals can simply choose not to be anxious, anxiety is not a conscious decision. It is rooted in intricate neurobiological processes and environmental influences. Recognizing anxiety as a nuanced experience promotes empathy and erases the burden of guilt associated with the misconception of it being a choice.

Myth: Anxiety Is Always Visible

Truth: Anxiety can manifest in ways that are not always externally apparent.

Anxiety doesn't always wear a visible mask. Internal struggles, emotional turmoil, and subtle behavioral changes may be indicative of anxiety. Understanding that anxiety can manifest in various forms, including hidden struggles, fosters a more inclusive and empathetic perspective.

Myth: Anxiety Is Just Excessive Worrying

Truth: Anxiety encompasses a spectrum of emotional, physical, and behavioral symptoms.

While excessive worrying is a common manifestation, anxiety goes beyond this singular dimension. It encompasses a spectrum of symptoms, including physical sensations, emotional turbulence, and behavioral changes. By broadening our understanding, we can better recognize and address the diverse facets of anxiety.

Myth: Anxiety Is Uncommon

Truth: Anxiety is a widespread and prevalent mental health concern.

Contrary to the misconception that anxiety is rare, it is, in fact, a pervasive mental health issue. According to the World Health Organization, millions of people worldwide grapple with anxiety disorders. Acknowledging its prevalence diminishes isolation and encourages open conversations surrounding mental health.

Evidence-Based Insights: Nurturing Understanding

To debunk myths effectively, we turn to evidence-based insights that illuminate the true nature of anxiety:

Biological Basis: Anxiety has a strong biological foundation, involving intricate interactions within the brain and nervous system. Neurotransmitters, hormones, and genetic factors contribute to the development and expression of anxiety.

Environmental Influences: Life experiences, trauma, and environmental stressors play a significant role in triggering and exacerbating anxiety. Understanding these influences fosters a compassionate approach to those navigating the complexities of anxiety.

Diverse Manifestations: Anxiety manifests differently in individuals, encompassing a wide range of symptoms. These may include cognitive distortions, physical sensations, and behavioral changes. Recognizing this diversity enhances our ability to identify and address anxiety comprehensively.

Reassurance and Hope: Embracing a Positive Outlook

Dispelling fears surrounding anxiety requires a touch of reassurance and a beacon of hope. Here's a compassionate affirmation:

You are not defined by your anxiety; it is a part of your journey, not the entirety of it. By seeking understanding, embracing self-compassion, and accessing supportive resources, you empower yourself to navigate the challenges of anxiety with resilience and hope. Your journey toward well-being is unique, and with each step, you move closer to a life marked by peace, balance, and fulfillment.

Embrace Authenticity:

Debunking myths about anxiety is a pivotal step toward fostering a culture of understanding and support. By embracing evidence-based insights and offering reassurance, we illuminate the path toward empowerment and healing. Anxiety, when viewed through the lens of truth and compassion, becomes a landscape where individuals can navigate with resilience and hope, dismantling fears and embracing the possibility of a brighter, more empowered future.

Chapter 2: Building a Foundation for Change

Begin by accepting anxiety as the first step towards overcoming it, emphasizing commitment and self-improvement. Develop self-awareness to target interventions, explore mindfulness for anxiety management, and learn effective breathing techniques. Establish the importance of a support system, offering tips for building and maintaining one, backed by real-life stories illustrating its impact on anxiety navigation.

Acceptance: A Prelude to Transformation:

Visualize acceptance as the tender dawn heralding the sunrise of change—a gentle warmth that permeates the soul. In the intricate tapestry of personal development, recognizing anxiety is not a surrender; rather, it's an intentional embrace—a conscious decision to comprehend, delve into, and ultimately transcend its grip. Acceptance acts as the compass steering us through the maze of self-discovery, urging us to be present with our struggles devoid of judgment.

Acceptance is not a passive act; it's an active engagement with our reality. It is the acknowledgment that each facet of our journey, including anxiety, contributes to the intricate mosaic of our being. It's about meeting ourselves where we are, understanding that the terrain of self-discovery is varied and nuanced.

As we navigate the landscape of acceptance, we encounter the healing power of acknowledgment. This acknowledgment is not a mere recognition; it's a profound embrace of our vulnerabilities and imperfections. It is the willingness to face our fears and uncertainties with compassion, fostering an environment where self-judgment withers away. Acknowledgment serves as a healing elixir, calming the wounds of self-judgment.

The essence of acknowledgment lies in its transformative potential. By empowering individuals through acknowledgment, anxiety loses its potency to fester in the shadows. This isn't a passive resignation but an empowered stance—an acknowledgment that lays the foundation for authentic transformation. It's a conscious choice to step into the light of self-awareness, allowing the healing rays to illuminate the darkest corners of our psyche.

Commitment: A Pledge to Your Genuine Self:

Built on the bedrock of acceptance, commitment emerges as the heartbeat of change—a rhythmic vow echoing the potential for transformation. It's not a rigid pact but a dynamic vow to self-improvement—a commitment to embark on the transformative journey with unwavering dedication. Each decision becomes a step toward a more authentic and resilient version of oneself, shaping the narrative of personal evolution.

Commitment is a deliberate choice to engage in the process of change. It is the recognition that change is not a destination but a continuous journey—one marked by growth, self-discovery, and evolving perspectives. In the realm of commitment, every choice becomes a brushstroke on the canvas of personal transformation.

To fully understand commitment, envision it as a dynamic force—a pulsating energy that propels us forward even when faced with challenges. It's not about avoiding difficulties but about embracing them with the unwavering belief that they are stepping stones on the path to personal evolution. Commitment is not a static state but a fluid dance with the rhythm of life.

Inspiration to Propel Transformation:

Standing on the threshold of change, let these motivational quotes and stories seamlessly kindle the flame of commitment within you, propelling you forward on this profound expedition.

"The only way to achieve the impossible is to believe it is possible." - *Charles Kingsleigh*

In the realm of self-improvement, belief is the cornerstone. Commitment thrives when anchored in the unwavering belief that change is not only possible but inevitable. Embrace this truth as a guiding mantra on your path to overcoming anxiety. Let belief be the wind beneath the wings of your commitment, carrying you toward the horizon of positive transformation.

"Success is not final, failure is not fatal: It is the courage to continue that counts." - *Winston Churchill*

Commitment is not immune to challenges, setbacks, or the ebb and flow of life. In the words of Winston Churchill, success is not the end, and failure is not the abyss. Instead, it's the courage to persevere through every note of the symphony that defines the journey. Let this wisdom be your anchor when facing the inevitable challenges on your path. The courage to continue is the heartbeat of commitment—a rhythmic cadence that echoes through the chapters of personal evolution.

The Parable of the Butterfly: A Metaphor for Metamorphosis

Envision a caterpillar cocooned in its comfort zone, resistant to change. Yet, within that chrysalis lies the transformative process birthing a butterfly. Commitment is the caterpillar's decision to embrace the discomfort of change, knowing that the wings of transformation will unfold. Allow this parable to remind you that commitment is the vessel through which profound metamorphosis occurs.

Commitment, like the caterpillar's decision to weave itself into the cocoon, involves a conscious choice to step into the discomfort of growth. It's an acknowledgment that change requires effort, persistence, and a willingness to undergo the transformative process. Just as the butterfly emerges with vibrant wings, commitment unfolds the hidden potential within us, revealing a more resilient and authentic self.

"You are never too old to set another goal or to dream a new dream." - C.S. Lewis

Commitment is not bound by time or circumstance. It is the perennial flame that can be ignited at any moment, regardless of where you stand in life. Let the words of C.S. Lewis be a beacon, encouraging you to set new goals, dream new dreams, and commit to the continuous evolution of your authentic self. The canvas of life is ever-expansive, and commitment is the brush that paints new dreams onto its surface.

Embrace Positive Change:

As you absorb the wisdom within these quotes and stories, may they resonate with the core of your being, sparking a flame of commitment that illuminates your journey toward a life of purpose, resilience, and enduring fulfillment. With each step guided by acceptance and commitment, you pave the way for a symphony of positive change to resonate throughout your existence.

In the symphony of change, acceptance and commitment are the harmonious notes that create a melody of transformation. The acceptance of where you are and the commitment to where you want to be form a powerful composition, guiding you through the ever-changing landscape of personal evolution. It's not just a chapter; it's a symphony—the orchestration of your journey toward a more authentic and fulfilling life.

Developing Self-Awareness for Lasting Transformation

Navigating the Profundities of Self-Awareness:

Embarking on a transformative odyssey into the heart of change, guided by the beacon of self-awareness, becomes an intricate dance with the inner self. It is an essential element that beckons us to explore the intricacies of our thoughts, emotions, and behaviors with a spirit of genuine curiosity and compassion. Let's commence this profound journey of self-discovery, immersing ourselves in purposeful exercises meticulously crafted to illuminate the subtle nuances of our inner landscape.

In the realm of personal transformation, envision self-awareness as the compass that steers the course through uncharted waters. It is not merely an intellectual understanding but a visceral connection with the symphony of one's own existence. This connection is the fertile ground from which meaningful change blossoms. As we set sail on this odyssey, we invite you to let the gentle waves of self-awareness carry you into the depths of your inner world.

Journeying Through Anxiety with Journaling:

The practice of maintaining an Anxiety Journal emerges as a sacred sanctuary, a reflective chronicle where thoughts and emotions unfurl without judgment. This journal is not merely a record but a living narrative of your internal landscape. Each day becomes a canvas, and your entries paint the strokes of heightened anxiety, capturing not only the context but also the intricate emotions they evoke.

In the silent dialogue between pen and paper, you become the storyteller and the witness. The Anxiety Journal transcends the mundane task of documentation; it transforms into a mirror, reflecting patterns and triggers that might otherwise remain concealed in the recesses of our consciousness. This introspective voyage becomes a means to unveil the untold tales of anxiety, allowing you to read between the lines of your own narrative.

Clarifying Life's Guiding Constellations:

Our values act as guiding constellations, casting light upon the vast expanse of our life journey. However, anxiety can cast shadows on these values, distorting their clarity and dimming their brilliance. Engaging in the Values Illumination Exercise becomes an act of stargazing within, where you list your core values and contemplate how anxiety may sway your alignment with them.

This exercise is not a theoretical exploration but a cosmic journey into the depths of your belief system. It unveils the impact of anxiety on your fundamental beliefs, paving the way for conscious realignment. As you navigate through the constellations of your values, you become an astronomer of your own existence, charting the celestial map that guides you through the cosmic dance of life.

Navigating the Emotional Terrain of Goals:

Goals, like constellations in the night sky, serve as waypoints on our life journey, subtly influenced by the cosmic forces of anxiety. Crafting an Aspirational Map transcends the realm of goal-setting; it becomes a cartographic endeavor delineating your short and long-term aspirations. Delve into the emotional landscape surrounding these goals, exploring how anxiety may be shaping your pursuit.

This cartography is not about charting geographical locations but mapping the emotional terrain of your aspirations. Unearth these connections for profound self-awareness, creating a map that not only guides you through the terrain of your aspirations but also serves as a compass in the cosmic journey of self-discovery.

Unveiling the Echoes of Anxiety on Values and Goals:

As we traverse through these exercises, the profound insights that emerge become ripples in the pond of self-awareness. Anxiety, much like a pebble dropped into a pond, generates ripples touching every aspect of our being. These ripples are not mere disturbances; they are echoes carrying the whispers of our internal symphony.

Each insight becomes a ripple that reaches the shores of self-discovery. These insights become stepping stones leading to targeted interventions—tools meticulously designed to recalibrate our inner symphony. In the ripple effect, we find the resonance of transformation, where the echoes of awareness create a harmonious melody within.

The Crossroads of Anxiety and Values:

Examine the intersection of anxiety and values revealed in your journal entries. This crossroads is not merely a point on the map; it is the convergence of cosmic energies shaping your existence. Are there values consistently challenged or compromised during anxious episodes? Acknowledge this crossroads as a focal point for intervention, where aligning with your values becomes a compass guiding you through moments of distress.

This intersection is not a static point but a dynamic interchange where the forces of anxiety and values meet. It is the nucleus of targeted interventions, the epicenter of self-awareness.

Navigating this intersection becomes an art—an art of aligning with the cosmic forces that guide you toward authenticity and resilience.

Goal Refinement in the Face of Anxiety:

Explore the emotional nuances surrounding your goals as if sculpting the aspirations that rise like mountain peaks in the cosmic landscape of your life. Are there aspirations tainted by anxiety-induced fears or self-doubt? Use this heightened awareness to reformulate your goals, infusing them with resilience and authenticity. Let self-awareness be the sculptor, reshaping your aspirations to withstand the winds of anxiety and stand resilient in the face of cosmic challenges.

The sculpting of goals becomes an artistic expression of self-awareness, where each stroke is guided by the celestial brush of understanding. In the vast canvas of your life, anxiety becomes a collaborator, not an antagonist. The sculpted aspirations become monuments that withstand the cosmic forces, representing the enduring spirit cultivated through self-awareness.

Embrace Awareness:

As we delve deeper into the symphony of self-awareness, we recognize it as the prelude to targeted interventions—an orchestration of strategies tailored to address the unique cadence of your anxiety. This symphony is not a mere performance but a living, breathing entity that evolves with each note.

As you navigate the path illuminated by self-discovery, remember that awareness is not a destination but a continual process, evolving with each note of the symphony. The symphony of self-awareness is a harmonious melody, preparing the stage for the transformative interventions to come. In this symphony, you are both the conductor and the instrument, shaping the cadence of your existence with the awareness born from the cosmic dance within.

The Role of Mindfulness in Anxiety Management

In the vast landscape of anxiety management, mindfulness emerges as a beacon of tranquility—an artful practice that involves cultivating a heightened awareness of the present moment. It beckons individuals to embrace a non-judgmental acceptance of their thoughts and feelings, providing a resilient mindset that counters the turbulence of anxiety. As we embark on an extended exploration, let's delve deeper into the profound role of mindfulness in fostering harmony within the intricate symphony of our inner world.

The Dance of Presence: A Choreography of Awareness

Imagine mindfulness as a dance—an intricate choreography that allows us to navigate the twists and turns of the present moment with grace. It invites us to step into the rhythm of our breath, the music of the now, guiding us away from the cacophony of anxious thoughts. This dance of presence becomes a sanctuary, a place where the mind finds solace in the simplicity of being.

The Tapestry of Awareness: Weaving Threads of Mindfulness

In the journey of mindfulness, we are weavers, crafting a tapestry of awareness. Each thread represents a moment of conscious presence, intricately woven into the fabric of our daily lives. The practice extends beyond formal meditation, threading its way into mundane moments—sipping tea, feeling the warmth of sunlight, or listening to the rustle of leaves. The tapestry grows, embodying the richness of mindful living.

Guiding the Novice: Gentle Entry Points to Mindfulness for Beginners:

For those taking their initial steps into the world of mindfulness, the path may seem daunting. However, simple and accessible exercises can serve as gentle entry points. Let's delve into an expanded exploration of beginner-friendly exercises designed to introduce individuals to the enriching practice of mindfulness.

Breath Awareness Meditation: A Journey into the Ocean of Breath
- Begin by finding a comfortable and quiet space, where you can retreat into a moment of introspection.
- Close your eyes and let your attention rest on your breath, the rhythmic tide that ties you to the present.
- Inhale deeply, feeling the air filling your lungs with revitalizing energy.
- Exhale slowly, releasing any tension or apprehension with each breath.

- Should your mind wander, gently guide it back to the soothing cadence of your breath. In this extended exploration, consider the oceanic metaphor of breath—an expansive, rhythmic force that mirrors the vastness of mindfulness.

Body Scan Meditation: A Journey Through the Landscape of the Body and Breath
- Find a serene spot where you can either sit or lie down, allowing your body to settle into a relaxed position.
- Direct the focus of your attention to different parts of your body, starting from your toes and gradually progressing to the crown of your head.
- Observe any sensations, noting areas of tension or moments of relaxation in each segment.

Permit your breath to flow naturally as you seamlessly scan through each body part, fostering a connection between breath and bodily awareness. In this expanded exploration, envision the body scan as a journey through a diverse landscape, with each body part offering its own terrain of sensations and experiences.

Narratives of Success through Mindfulness:

Real-life narratives unfold as testimonials, revealing the transformative impact of mindfulness on the fabric of anxiety. Within these stories, we encounter individuals who have harnessed the calming influence of mindfulness practices to navigate the intricate terrain of anxiety. Let's extend our exploration into the profound narratives of Emma and Daniel.

Emma's Journey to Present Living: A Symphony of Transformation

Immersed in the perpetual stream of anxious thoughts, Emma embarked on a transformative journey into mindfulness. Through consistent and deliberate practice, she uncovered the profound power of being present. Mindfulness became her sanctuary—a space where she could observe her thoughts without the weight of judgment. In this expanded narrative, we unravel the symphony of Emma's transformation, exploring the nuanced notes that guided her from chaos to serenity.

Daniel's Breath as an Anchor: A Journey Through Calm Waters

Amidst the tumultuous waves of panic attacks, Daniel sought refuge in the simplicity of breath awareness meditation. By elevating this practice to a daily ritual, he discovered solace in the rhythmic dance of his breath. Mindfulness, for Daniel, became an anchor—a steadfast foundation that provided stability during moments of anxiety. In this extended narrative, we delve deeper into Daniel's journey, navigating the ebb and flow of his breath as a metaphor for resilience in the face of anxiety.

Mindfulness as a Guiding Light:

Mindfulness stands as a guiding light in the intricate journey of anxiety management. Its significance extends far beyond theoretical concepts, manifesting in practical exercises carefully crafted to empower beginners. As we further intertwine the wisdom of mindfulness with inspiring success stories, this section endeavors to illuminate the transformative path toward tranquility and presence in the face of anxiety.

The Wisdom Within Silence: Deepening the Practice of Mindfulness

As we delve further into the ocean of mindfulness, let silence become the companion on this journey. Silence, often overlooked, is the canvas on which the brushstrokes of mindfulness paint their vivid hues. In this extended exploration, we discover the wisdom that resides within the pauses—moments of profound stillness that amplify the impact of mindfulness on our inner world.

Embrace Mindful Living and Mindful Being

Mindfulness transcends exercises; it is a way of being. Let's broaden our understanding by exploring how mindfulness extends into the fabric of our daily lives—how we eat, engage in conversations, or simply savor the texture of the present moment. Mindful living is not a destination but a continual journey, and we invite you to join this expansive exploration.

As we navigate this extended exploration, let mindfulness be the compass that steers us through the waters of self-discovery. With each breath and every present moment, may we find solace in the gentle embrace of mindfulness—a practice that not only nurtures tranquility within but also lights the way toward a resilient and serene existence amidst the complexities of anxiety.

Navigating Acute Anxiety with Transformative Breathwork

In the intricate dance of managing anxiety, the breath emerges as a stalwart anchor—a guiding force capable of leading us back to the sanctuary of centeredness. Before we embark on the journey of breathing techniques, let's set the stage, appreciating the profound and transformative power of breath in the context of acute anxiety.

The breath, often taken for granted in the hustle and bustle of daily life, becomes a lifeline during moments of heightened anxiety. It serves as a bridge between the internal landscape of emotions and the external world, offering a tangible connection to the present moment. This introductory exploration aims to deepen our understanding of the breath's role as an anchor, a stabilizing force that weaves through the intricate tapestry of anxiety management.

Guided Breathing Practices for Tranquility: Lifelines in the Storm

As we navigate the stormy seas of acute anxiety, guided breathing practices emerge as lifelines—crafted with precision to bring calm amidst the relentless waves of emotions. Each breath becomes a rhythmic dance, a gentle current that guides us toward the shores of tranquility. Let's embark on an exploration of these techniques, envisioning each breath as a soothing wave in the vast ocean of emotional turbulence.

Box Breathing:

The Box Breathing technique unfolds as a series of deliberate steps, transforming each breath into a mindful journey. Inhale deeply, feeling the air fill your lungs, and hold your breath—a moment of suspended stillness. Exhale slowly, releasing tension, and pause—a brief interlude of quiet awareness. Repeat this rhythmic cycle, allowing the breath's cadence to guide you into a realm of calm awareness. Each count becomes a step on the staircase of serenity, leading you to the tranquil haven within.

4-7-8 Technique:

In the symphony of controlled breathing, the 4-7-8 technique resonates as a harmonious melody. Inhale quietly through your nose, drawing in tranquility with each breath. Hold your breath, savoring the serenity within, and exhale completely through your mouth—releasing stress and inviting calm. Repeat this cycle as needed, each breath a gentle reminder of relaxation and composure. The numbers become a rhythmic dance, orchestrating a soothing cadence that echoes through the chambers of your breath.

Diaphragmatic Breathing:

The diaphragm, a silent conductor in the orchestra of breath, takes center stage in this practice. Place one hand on your chest and the other on your abdomen, forging a connection with the center of breath. Inhale deeply through your nose, allowing your abdomen to expand with the life force of the breath. Exhale slowly through pursed lips, feeling your abdomen contract in a rhythmic dance of release. Focus on the diaphragmatic movement, each breath creating a deep, calming wave that washes over you. The breath becomes a dance partner, leading you through the steps of tranquility.

Whispers of Relief: Real-Life Testimonials on the Power of Controlled Breathing

As we transition into the realm of real-life testimonials, these narratives serve as echoes of relief—resonating with the immediate solace that controlled breathing can bring amidst the heightened symphony of anxiety. These stories become testaments to the universal and transformative potential of incorporating controlled breathing into the intricate dance of anxiety management.

Sophie's Calming Ritual:

Sophie's journey unfolds as a testament to the transformative impact of diaphragmatic breathing—a gentle ritual that became her sanctuary in the storm of overwhelming panic attacks. This practice, initially a lifeline, evolved into a calming ritual, providing a tangible and grounding anchor during moments of acute anxiety. Sophie's testimonial paints a vivid picture of the immediate relief that controlled breathing can offer—a lifeline in the storm of panic, a melody of calm in the chaos.

James' Journey to Composure:

In the tumultuous waves of generalized anxiety, James discovered the profound composure that the 4-7-8 breathing technique could instill. Through consistent practice, he experienced a shift in composure during anxious episodes, illustrating the empowering nature of controlled breathing. James' journey serves as a testament to the transformative potential of breath—a tool that not only manages acute anxiety but also cultivates resilience and inner strength. The rhythmic dance of controlled breathing becomes a powerful ally in navigating the complexities of anxiety.

Breathing as Empowerment: A Lifelong Companion

The power of breath emerges not as a fleeting tool but as a lifelong companion for managing acute anxiety. The guided practices presented here are not mere techniques; they are tools designed to empower readers with accessible and transformative breathwork they can seamlessly integrate into their daily lives. Through the lens of real-life testimonials, this section underscores the universal and timeless potential of controlled breathing—a practice that transcends the boundaries of anxiety, bringing moments of peace and calm to those who embrace its rhythmic dance.

Unveiling the Depth: A Deeper Dive into Breathwork and Anxiety

As we unravel the layers of breathwork in anxiety management, it's essential to delve deeper into the physiological and psychological dimensions of these practices. Understanding the intricate interplay between breath and the nervous system provides a foundation for embracing the full spectrum of breathwork's potential in anxiety relief.

Physiological Dimensions of Breathwork: Bridging the Mind-Body Connection

The breath, a bridge between the conscious and the subconscious, acts as a profound catalyst in regulating the autonomic nervous system. In moments of acute anxiety, the sympathetic nervous system, responsible for the fight-or-flight response, takes center stage. Controlled breathing techniques, such as those explored earlier, offer a tangible means of activating the parasympathetic nervous system—the body's natural calming mechanism.

When we engage in intentional and controlled breathing, the diaphragm, a primary muscle of respiration, plays a pivotal role. Diaphragmatic breathing, in particular, encourages deep, slow breaths, activating the vagus nerve. This activation initiates a cascade of responses, including the release of acetylcholine, a neurotransmitter known for its calming effect. The physiological dance of breath becomes a gateway to tranquility—a direct pathway to counteracting the physiological manifestations of anxiety.

Psychological Dimensions of Breathwork: A Journey into Mindful Awareness

Beyond the physiological realm, the practice of controlled breathing ventures into the landscape of mindful awareness. Mindfulness, a cornerstone of breathwork, involves cultivating a heightened awareness of the present moment with a non-judgmental acceptance of thoughts and feelings. The synergy between breath and mindfulness creates a harmonious resonance, offering individuals a toolkit to navigate the intricate terrain of their inner world.

In the midst of acute anxiety, thoughts often spiral into a whirlwind of worry, fear, and anticipation. The breath, a constant and reliable anchor, becomes a focal point for redirecting attention. Each inhale and exhale becomes an opportunity to ground oneself in the present moment, breaking the cycle of anxious thoughts. The rhythmic cadence of breath aligns with the rhythm of mindfulness, inviting individuals to witness their thoughts without judgment and with a compassionate curiosity.

Embarking on a Journey of Breathwork Exploration: Tailoring Techniques to Individual Needs

As we unveil the depth of breathwork's potential, it becomes evident that a one-size-fits-all approach may not fully harness its transformative power. Tailoring breathwork techniques to individual needs and preferences allows for a more personalized and resonant practice. This exploration involves embracing a variety of breathwork modalities, understanding their nuances, and integrating them into daily life based on individual circumstances.

Exploring Breathwork Modalities:

Breathwork encompasses a rich tapestry of modalities, each with its unique qualities and benefits. Exploring these modalities provides individuals with a palette of options to choose from, enabling them to discover the techniques that resonate most deeply with their personal experiences of anxiety. Let's delve into a few breathwork modalities, inviting readers to embark on a journey of exploration and self-discovery.

Pranayama: Ancient Wisdom Meets Modern Anxiety Management

Pranayama, an ancient yogic practice, translates to "extension of the life force" in Sanskrit. This breathwork modality involves conscious regulation of breath, emphasizing specific techniques to control the flow of prana or life energy within the body. Incorporating pranayama into anxiety management introduces individuals to a time-honored tradition that aligns breath with the subtle energies of the body.

Anulom Vilom, commonly known as alternate nostril breathing, stands out as a pranayama technique with potential benefits for anxiety relief. This practice involves alternating the inhalation and exhalation between the left and right nostrils, creating a sense of balance and harmony within the nervous system. As individuals engage in this rhythmic dance of breath, they may find a profound sense of centeredness and equilibrium.

Kapalabhati: The Breath of Fire for Energized Calmness

Kapalabhati, often referred to as the "Breath of Fire," is another pranayama technique that blends energizing breathwork with a calming influence. This technique involves rapid and forceful exhalations through the nose, followed by passive inhalations. The dynamic nature of Kapalabhati enlivens the body, increases oxygenation, and promotes mental clarity—a synthesis of invigoration and serenity.

Box Breathing: A Modern Twist on Timeless Wisdom

While box breathing has already been introduced as a guided breathing practice, its roots can be traced to ancient breathwork wisdom. Box breathing finds resonance in military and yogic traditions alike, showcasing the universality of breath as a transformative tool. Understanding its historical context enriches the practice, providing a bridge between ancient wisdom and contemporary applications.

Mindful Breathing: A Gateway to Present Living

Mindful breathing, rooted in contemplative traditions, transcends specific techniques to embrace a holistic approach to breathwork. At its core, mindful breathing involves bringing full awareness to each breath, savoring the inhalation and exhalation with a gentle attentiveness. The practice of mindful breathing aligns seamlessly with the principles of mindfulness, inviting individuals to be fully present with the unfolding moment.

Integrating Breathwork into Daily Life: Beyond Moments of Anxiety

The true essence of breathwork extends beyond moments of acute anxiety; it integrates into the fabric of daily life, becoming a companion in the journey of well-being. As individuals explore diverse breathwork modalities, incorporating them into daily routines fosters a continual sense of connection with the breath's transformative power. Let's delve into ways to seamlessly integrate breathwork into various facets of daily life, enhancing its accessibility and impact.

Morning Rituals: Cultivating Calm for the Day Ahead

Mornings, often a canvas for setting the tone of the day, offer an opportune moment to engage in breathwork rituals. Creating a morning routine that incorporates breathwork provides a foundation for resilience and centeredness. Here are a few suggestions for weaving breathwork into morning rituals:

- Wake-Up Breath: Before rising from bed, engage in a few minutes of mindful breathing. Connect with the breath, inhaling the freshness of a new day and exhaling any residual tension from sleep.
- Shower Breathing Meditation: Transform your morning shower into a mindful breathing meditation. Allow the sensation of water to become a metaphor for cleansing breath, inhaling positivity and exhaling any lingering concerns.
- Sun Salutation with Breath Awareness: If you engage in yoga or stretching exercises, synchronize breath awareness with movement. Inhale during stretches and exhale during contractions, creating a harmonious flow.
- Gratitude Breathing: As you prepare for the day, take a moment to express gratitude with each breath. Inhale gratitude for the opportunities ahead, and exhale gratitude for the present moment.

- Workday Integration: Breath Breaks for Productivity and Resilience

Amidst the demands of work, carving out brief moments for breath breaks contributes to enhanced productivity and resilience. Integrating breathwork into the workday offers a reprieve from stressors and fosters a focused and composed mindset. Consider the following strategies for seamlessly infusing breathwork into your work routine:

- Desk Breathing Exercises: Schedule brief intervals throughout the day for desk-based breathing exercises. Whether it's box breathing or diaphragmatic breathing, these moments of intentional breathwork can rejuvenate your mind and body.
- Commute Breathing Practice: Transform your commute, whether by car or public transportation, into an opportunity for breathwork. Engage in mindful breathing, using the rhythm of travel as a backdrop for centering yourself.
- Meeting Mindfulness: Begin or conclude meetings with a collective moment of mindfulness and breath awareness. This practice fosters a shared sense of presence and can enhance the overall atmosphere of collaboration.
- Lunchtime Rejuvenation: During your lunch break, step away from your workspace and find a quiet spot. Engage in a rejuvenating breathwork session to reset your energy for the remainder of the day. Mindful breathing during lunch can serve as a bridge between the morning's activities and the tasks that lie ahead, promoting a sense of balance and clarity.

Afternoon Uplift: Nurturing Well-Being Amidst Responsibilities

As the day unfolds, the demands of work and personal responsibilities may intensify. Incorporating breathwork into the afternoon can act as a source of sustenance, offering a moment of reprieve from the hustle and bustle. Consider these breathwork practices to nurture your well-being during the afternoon:

Mindful Walking Breaths:

Take a short break for a mindful walk, and synchronize your breath with each step. Inhale deeply for a few steps, hold your breath briefly, and exhale slowly. Allow the rhythm of your breath to harmonize with your steps, bringing a sense of calm and focus.

Three-Part Breath:

Find a comfortable seated position. Inhale deeply into your abdomen, allowing it to expand. Continue inhaling, filling your chest, and finally, your upper lungs. Exhale slowly in reverse order. This three-part breath engages your entire respiratory system, promoting relaxation and heightened awareness.

Desk Yoga Breath Flow:

Incorporate gentle yoga stretches into your afternoon routine, combining breath awareness with movement. Flow through seated yoga poses, coordinating each movement with your breath. This practice can release tension accumulated during desk work and invigorate your body and mind.

Breathwork for Task Transition:

Before transitioning between tasks or projects, take a moment for intentional breathwork. Inhale deeply to gather focus and exhale to release any lingering tension. This brief pause prepares your mind for the upcoming challenge, promoting a smoother transition.

Evening Unwinding: Harnessing Breath for Restful Nights

As the evening approaches, transitioning from the demands of the day to a state of relaxation is crucial for a restful night's sleep. Breathwork can be a powerful tool to unwind and signal to your body that it's time to shift into a more tranquil state. Consider incorporating these breathwork practices into your evening routine:

Nightly Reflection Breath:

Find a quiet space before bedtime. Reflect on the day's events and emotions. Inhale to embrace positive moments, exhale to release any negativity. This reflective breath promotes a sense of closure, allowing you to let go of the day's stressors.

4-7-8 Evening Calm:

Lie down comfortably and practice the 4-7-8 breathing technique. Inhale for a count of four, hold for seven counts, and exhale for eight counts. This rhythmic breathing signals to your nervous system that it's time to unwind, promoting a sense of calmness.

Guided Body Relaxation:

Combine breath awareness with a guided body relaxation exercise. Inhale to a specific body part, exhale to release tension from that area. Gradually move through each part of your body, promoting overall relaxation and preparing your body for a restful sleep.

Embrace the Breath's Ever-Present Rhythm

In summary, weaving breathwork into your daily routine offers a multifaceted approach to managing anxiety and enhancing overall well-being. Morning rituals set the tone for the day, workday integration sustains resilience, afternoon practices nurture well-being, and evening unwinding prepares the mind and body for restful sleep.

The breath, often taken for granted, emerges as a lifelong companion—a reliable anchor amidst the ebb and flow of daily life. The rhythmic dance of inhalations and exhalations becomes a melody guiding you through moments of heightened anxiety, stress, and serenity. As you embrace the transformative power of breath, you embark on a journey towards a harmonious and centered existence, where the breath's ever-present rhythm becomes a testament to your inner resilience and well-being.

The Pillars of Support: Foundations of Emotional Well-being

Before we delve into the practical aspects of constructing and nurturing a support system, let's explore the foundational pillars that underpin this network. Just as a sturdy structure relies on robust pillars for support, a resilient support system becomes the bedrock of emotional well-being. Understanding the significance of these pillars is paramount for cultivating a network that stands firm during challenging times.

Understanding the Pillars:

To truly grasp the essence of support systems, let's delve into an in-depth exploration of the fundamental pillars that contribute to their strength:

Empathy as the Cornerstone:

Empathy forms the cornerstone of any meaningful support system. It is the ability to understand and share the feelings of another. In a supportive relationship, the empathetic pillar provides a strong foundation for emotional connection and mutual understanding.

Trust as the Binding Force:

Trust is the binding force that holds the pillars together. It is built through consistent reliability, honesty, and confidentiality. A support system characterized by trust allows individuals to be vulnerable, knowing that their thoughts and feelings are secure within the confines of the network.

Understanding Through Active Listening:

Active listening is the bridge that connects individuals within a support system. It involves fully concentrating, understanding, responding, and remembering what is being said. This pillar ensures that the nuances of one's experience are acknowledged and validated.

Shared Values and Beliefs:

The alignment of values and beliefs creates a shared ground within the support system. When individuals within the network resonate with similar principles, it strengthens the connection and facilitates a harmonious exchange of support.

Tips for Cultivating and Sustaining Your Support System: A Continuous Journey

Building and maintaining a support system is an ongoing process that demands intentionality and care. Here are practical tips to guide you on this transformative journey:

Identify Your Supportive Circle:

> Reflect on the individuals in your life who have consistently shown empathy and understanding. This circle may encompass friends, family, colleagues, or support groups—individuals who contribute positively to your overall well-being.

Communicate Your Needs:

> Open and honest communication serves as the cornerstone of a strong support system. Clearly articulate your needs, boundaries, and preferences to those within your support network. Effective communication establishes a foundation of understanding and trust.

Reciprocity in Relationships:

> Support is a reciprocal exchange. Cultivate relationships where both parties feel valued and supported. This mutual give-and-take fosters a sense of community, strengthening the bonds within your support network.

Diversify Your Support Sources:

> Relying on a variety of support sources ensures a well-rounded and resilient network. Different individuals may provide unique perspectives, forms of assistance, and coping mechanisms. Diversification enriches the supportive landscape.

Stories Illuminating the Impact of Support Systems:

Let's transition into real-life narratives that serve as testaments to the transformative impact of support systems in the realm of anxiety. These stories unfold the diverse ways in which supportive relationships can become steadfast anchors amid the storm of anxiety:

Anna's Healing Circle:

> Anna, grappling with the challenges of social anxiety, discovered solace in a close-knit group of friends. These friends actively participated in her exposure exercises, offering unwavering support. Their collective commitment became a healing circle, contributing significantly to Anna's gradual triumph over social anxiety.

David's Family Resilience:

David, confronting panic disorder, leaned on his family for emotional validation and practical support. Their collective resilience formed a familial safety net, enabling David to navigate the complexities of panic attacks with greater ease. The family's support became a crucial element in David's journey toward healing.

The Pillars in Action: Realizing the Transformative Power

Understanding the theoretical aspects of support system pillars is crucial, but witnessing them in action provides a deeper insight into their transformative power. Let's explore how each pillar manifests in real-life scenarios, amplifying its impact:

Empathy Unveiled: A Beacon of Understanding:

In moments of distress, empathy acts as a beacon, guiding individuals toward understanding and connection. When a friend empathetically acknowledges the challenges someone faces with anxiety, it creates a space where vulnerability is met with compassion.

Trust as the Solid Ground:

Picture a support system built on trust as a solid ground where individuals feel secure to share their innermost thoughts and fears. Trust allows for open conversations without the fear of judgment, fostering an environment conducive to emotional well-being.

Active Listening as a Form of Validation:

Active listening becomes a form of validation, demonstrating that one's experiences are not only heard but truly understood. In a support system characterized by active listening, individuals feel seen and validated in their struggles, contributing to a sense of worth and acknowledgment.

Shared Values and Beliefs in Action:

Witness the power of shared values and beliefs when a support system rallies around a common cause. Whether it's participating in advocacy work, promoting mental health awareness, or simply sharing common interests, this shared ground becomes a unifying force within the support network.

Crafting Resilience Through Connection

The process of building and maintaining a robust support system can be likened to weaving a tapestry of resilience. This intricate fabric, woven with threads of understanding, empathy, and practical assistance, becomes a source of strength during the turbulent moments of anxiety.

As you embark on the journey of creating your support network, envision each relationship as a thread contributing to the overall resilience of the tapestry. Every connection shapes a supportive environment where you can navigate the symphony of anxiety with greater ease and fortitude. Remember, the tapestry is dynamic and ever-evolving, mirroring the growth and adaptability inherent in a well-nurtured support system.

Evolving the Tapestry: Sustaining Growth and Adaptability

To sustain the growth and adaptability of the supportive tapestry, consider these strategies:

Regular Check-ins:

> Establish a routine for regular check-ins within your support system. These check-ins can be virtual or in-person meetings where individuals share updates, challenges, and victories. Consistent communication nurtures the evolving connections.

Educational Endeavors:

> Foster a culture of continuous learning within your support network. This could involve attending workshops, reading relevant literature, or engaging in activities that promote mutual understanding of mental health and well-being.

Celebrating Milestones:

> Take the time to celebrate individual and collective milestones within the support system. Recognizing achievements, whether big or small, reinforces a positive and uplifting atmosphere.

Flexibility and Adaptation:

> Recognize that the dynamics of life and relationships change. Be open to adapting the structure of your support system to accommodate these changes. Flexibility ensures the tapestry remains resilient and responsive to evolving needs.

Embracing Vulnerability: Strengthening the Threads

Vulnerability is the essence of connection, and within a support system, it serves as the glue that strengthens the threads of the tapestry. Encourage open conversations about vulnerabilities, fears, and challenges. This shared vulnerability deepens the bonds and creates an environment where individuals feel safe to express their authentic selves.

The Ripple Effect: Impact Beyond the Individual

As your support system flourishes and evolves, its positive impact extends beyond individual well-being. The ripple effect encompasses the broader community, fostering a culture of empathy, understanding, and mental health awareness. The supportive tapestry you weave becomes a testament to the transformative power of connection.

Cultivating Support for All: Inclusivity in Support Networks

In cultivating a support system, it's essential to consider inclusivity. Acknowledge and celebrate diversity within your network, recognizing that each individual brings unique perspectives and experiences. An inclusive support system embraces differences and ensures that everyone feels valued and heard.

Expanding the Tapestry: Connecting Communities

Consider expanding the tapestry of your support system to connect with broader communities. Engage in initiatives that promote mental health advocacy, community outreach, and the stigmatization of mental health challenges. By connecting with external communities, you contribute to a more supportive and understanding society.

Embrace Connection

The journey of building and maintaining a support system unfolds as a continuous tapestry of resilience and connection. Each thread represents a relationship, an experience, and a shared commitment to emotional well-being. As you navigate the symphony of anxiety, may the tapestry you weave become a source of strength, comfort, and inspiration.

Remember that the tapestry is a living entity, evolving with time and experiences. Nurture its growth, celebrate its diversity, and cherish the connections that form its intricate patterns. In the tapestry of support, you find not only solace amid life's challenges but also the transformative power of human connection.

Chapter 3: Cognitive Approaches to Managing Anxiety

Learn techniques for thought challenging and reframing, supported by real-life scenarios demonstrating effective thought restructuring. Acquire problem-solving skills to address anxiety-inducing situations through practical exercises and impactful stories. Finally, delve into building cognitive resilience, discovering daily practices, fostering a resilient mindset in the face of life's challenges.

Unraveling the Intricate Threads of Thought

Within the intricate tapestry of anxiety management, our thoughts emerge as master weavers, crafting a powerful narrative that shapes our mental landscape. This section serves as a lantern, guiding us through the shadows of cognitive approaches—a journey to unveil the subtle distortions that often fuel the flames of anxiety.

At the core of this exploration lies the unraveling of cognitive distortions, those subtle twists that tint our perception of reality. Imagine them as whispers that, when left unexamined, can escalate into roars of anxiety. The comprehension of these distortions marks the initial stride toward reclaiming command over our mental canvas.

The Dance Between Thoughts and Anxiety:

Each thought pattern serves as a brushstroke on the canvas of our emotional experience. By dissecting this connection, we gain insight into how specific distortions amplify anxiety, setting the stage for effective interventions.

Examples of Common Distortions:

Catastrophizing:

> Envision the mind's inclination to conjure catastrophic scenarios out of ordinary events. It's an art form that paints a canvas of anxiety, overshadowing the hues of reality.

All-or-Nothing Thinking:

> Picture a world painted in extremes—where situations are either all good or all bad. This distortion limits the nuances of perception, fostering anxiety through polarized perspectives.

Overgeneralization:

Peer into the habit of drawing sweeping conclusions based on limited evidence. It's a distortion that casts a shadow on future experiences, contributing to sustained anxiety.

Personalization:

Explore the tendency to attribute external events to oneself, assuming an undue responsibility that fuels anxiety. Unravel the threads of personalization and liberate yourself from the weight of unwarranted guilt.

Counter-Strategies: Crafting a Resilient Narrative

Empower yourself with counter-strategies that reshape the narratives crafted by cognitive distortions.

Mindful Reframing:

Cultivate mindfulness as a potent ally in reframing distorted thoughts. Mindfulness invites you to step back, observe thoughts without judgment, and consciously reframe them with a balanced perspective. Practice mindfulness not as a cure but as a continual process of awareness and reframing.

Thought Restructuring:

Engage in thought restructuring exercises to challenge distorted thinking. This involves identifying, evaluating, and replacing negative thoughts with more realistic and balanced alternatives. Consider creating a structured plan for thought restructuring, incorporating it into your daily routine to build a resilient cognitive framework.

Gratitude Practice:

Infuse your daily routine with gratitude. This simple yet profound practice disrupts patterns of negativity, fostering a mindset that counters distortions and reduces anxiety. Develop a gratitude journal where you document moments of appreciation, creating a tangible reminder of positivity in your life.

Exercises for Liberation:

Thought Journaling:

Initiate a Thought Journal—a sacred space to document anxious thoughts, their distortions, and alternative, balanced perspectives. This practice becomes a compass, guiding you through the intricate maze of cognitive patterns. Dedicate time regularly to reflect on your journal, recognizing patterns and refining your awareness.

Reality Testing:

Engage in reality testing exercises to objectively evaluate the evidence supporting anxious thoughts. This process unveils the disparities between distorted perceptions and actual circumstances, empowering you to challenge their validity. Practice reality testing in real-time situations, applying critical thinking to untangle distorted thoughts.

Mindful Moments:

Incorporate mindfulness into your daily life. Whether through focused breathing or grounding exercises, these mindful moments interrupt the cycle of distorted thinking, offering clarity and calm. Design a personalized mindfulness routine, experimenting with different techniques to discover what resonates best with you.

Affirmation Integration:

Integrate positive affirmations into your daily rituals. Develop a repertoire of affirmations that counter specific distortions. Repeat these affirmations regularly, embedding them into your subconscious mind to overwrite negative thought patterns.

As you embark on this journey of unraveling cognitive distortions, remember that awareness is the cornerstone of transformation. By understanding the intricacies of your thoughts, you pave the way for a more resilient and balanced mental landscape—a landscape where anxiety loses its foothold, and you regain control of your narrative. The richness of this exploration lies not just in the understanding of distortions but in the ongoing commitment to implement counter-strategies that lead to lasting change.

Navigating the Emotional Tapestry:

While cognitive approaches offer valuable insights into managing anxiety, they constitute just one facet of the intricate emotional landscapes we traverse. Beyond the realm of cognitive distortions, our emotional experiences are shaped by a multitude of factors, including past traumas, interpersonal dynamics, and environmental influences. Recognizing the interconnectedness of these elements provides a comprehensive perspective on anxiety management.

There are interwoven threads that compose the elaborate tapestry of our emotional experiences. By navigating these landscapes, we not only deepen our understanding of the roots of anxiety but also empower ourselves to cultivate emotional resilience.

Our emotional landscapes bear the imprints of past experiences, resonating through the corridors of memory. To navigate these landscapes effectively, we must trace the threads of the past, unraveling the influences that shape our emotional responses. Consider employing the following strategies:

Reflective Journaling:

Commence a Reflective Journal—a tool designed for exploring past experiences and understanding their emotional impact. Through introspective writing, trace the threads of your past, identifying pivotal moments that contribute to present emotional patterns.

Therapeutic Exploration:

Engage in therapeutic exploration with a trained professional. Therapeutic modalities, such as psychotherapy or counseling, provide a structured space to delve into the depths of past experiences, fostering healing and understanding.

Artistic Expression:

Explore artistic avenues as a means to express and process emotions. Art, whether through writing, drawing, or other creative outlets, serves as a medium for untangling emotional threads and gaining insight into their origins. Allow your creativity to guide you through the intricate maze of your emotional landscape.

The Interplay of Interpersonal Dynamics:

Our interactions with others create a dynamic tapestry of emotions, influencing our mental and emotional well-being. Understanding the interplay of interpersonal dynamics is essential for fostering healthy relationships and mitigating anxiety triggers.

Communication Styles:

Explore different communication styles and their impact on emotional exchanges. Assess your own communication patterns and identify areas for improvement. Cultivate open and assertive communication, creating a supportive environment that minimizes misunderstandings and reduces anxiety.

Boundaries and Relationships:

Reflect on your boundaries within relationships. Establishing clear and healthy boundaries is crucial for maintaining emotional well-being. Evaluate the reciprocity of boundaries in your relationships, ensuring a balance that nurtures mutual respect and understanding.

Supportive Networks:

Cultivate supportive networks that extend beyond cognitive approaches. These networks, comprising friends, family, or support groups, contribute to emotional resilience. Strengthening interpersonal connections creates a safety net of emotional support during challenging times.

Environmental Influences: Cultivating Nourishing Spaces

Our physical environment plays a significant role in shaping emotional well-being. Creating nourishing spaces within our surroundings contributes to a sense of safety and calm. Consider the following strategies:

Decluttering:

Begin with decluttering your physical space. A clutter-free environment fosters mental clarity and reduces sensory overload, contributing to a calmer emotional state. Dedicate time regularly to organize and simplify your living spaces.

Nature Connection:

Cultivate a connection with nature. Spending time outdoors, whether in parks, gardens, or natural settings, has a rejuvenating effect on emotional well-being. Incorporate nature walks or outdoor activities into your routine to refresh your mind and spirit.

Mindful Living Spaces:

Infuse mindfulness into your living spaces. Create areas that promote relaxation and contemplation, such as a meditation corner or a cozy reading nook. Mindful living spaces serve as retreats where you can recharge and find solace.

The Intersection of Cognitive and Emotional Approaches

As we navigate the intricate terrain of cognitive and emotional landscapes, it's crucial to recognize their intersection. Cognitive approaches provide tools for understanding and reshaping thought patterns, while emotional exploration delves into the deeper roots of our feelings. The synergy of these approaches forms a comprehensive strategy for anxiety management.

Cognitive-Emotional Integration Practices

Mindful Cognitive Restructuring:

Combine mindfulness with cognitive restructuring. Practice mindful awareness of cognitive distortions as they arise, and use mindfulness techniques to anchor yourself in the present moment. This integration enhances your ability to respond to distorted thoughts with clarity and calm.

Emotional Awareness Journal:

Create an Emotional Awareness Journal—a tool for tracking both cognitive and emotional patterns. Record moments of heightened anxiety, identifying the thoughts and emotions that coincide. This journal becomes a bridge between cognitive and emotional exploration, offering a comprehensive view of your internal landscape.

Visualization for Emotional Resilience:

Incorporate visualization techniques to enhance emotional resilience. Visualize scenarios that typically trigger anxiety, applying cognitive strategies to reframe thoughts and emotions. Visualization serves as a proactive tool for preparing your mind to navigate challenging situations.

Collaborative Therapeutic Approaches:

Engage in therapeutic approaches that seamlessly blend cognitive and emotional modalities. Collaborative therapeutic practices, such as cognitive-behavioral therapy (CBT) or dialectical behavior therapy (DBT), offer a unified framework for addressing cognitive distortions and emotional responses.

Balancing the Cognitive-Emotional Scale

Achieving balance between cognitive and emotional approaches is a dynamic process. It involves ongoing self-reflection, adaptive strategies, and a commitment to nurturing both aspects of our internal world. Consider the following principles for maintaining this equilibrium:

Regular Self-Reflection:

Dedicate time for regular self-reflection. Create a reflective practice that integrates cognitive and emotional exploration. Use this time to assess your thought patterns, emotional responses, and the interplay between the two.

Adaptive Strategy Implementation:

Be adaptable in your approach. Recognize that strategies effective in one context may need adjustment in another. Embrace flexibility, allowing your cognitive and emotional approaches to evolve based on the nuances of each situation.

Compassionate Self-Acceptance:

Cultivate compassionate self-acceptance. Acknowledge that both cognitive distortions and emotional responses are inherent aspects of the human experience. Approach your internal world with kindness and curiosity, fostering an environment conducive to growth.

Holistic Well-Being Focus:

Shift your focus toward holistic well-being. Anxiety management extends beyond the alleviation of symptoms—it encompasses the cultivation of a balanced and thriving life. Prioritize practices that contribute to physical, mental, and emotional well-being.

Navigating Relapses with Resilience

Despite our best efforts, anxiety may resurface, challenging the equilibrium we've cultivated. Navigating relapses with resilience involves recognizing them as opportunities for deeper understanding and growth. Consider the following strategies:

Deconstructing Relapses:

Approach relapses with a mindset of curiosity. Deconstruct the factors contributing to the relapse, exploring both cognitive triggers and emotional influences. This process unveils insights that can inform future strategies.

Adjusting Cognitive Tools:

If cognitive tools prove less effective during a relapse, be open to adjustment. Explore alternative cognitive strategies or modify existing ones to better align with the current emotional landscape. Flexibility in your cognitive toolkit enhances its relevance over time.

Emotional Exploration in Relapse:

Use relapses as opportunities for emotional exploration. Dive into the emotional undercurrents accompanying anxiety, employing cognitive-emotional integration practices. This depth of exploration contributes to lasting resilience.

Seeking Support:

During relapses, lean on your support system. Communicate openly with those in your supportive circle, expressing your needs and challenges. Social support becomes a crucial anchor during challenging times, offering perspectives and insights that contribute to resilience.

Embrace Self-Discovery

The journey of anxiety management unfolds as a dynamic exploration of self-discovery. The interplay between cognitive and emotional approaches forms the tapestry of our internal landscapes, intricately woven with threads of awareness, resilience, and growth.

As you navigate this journey, embrace the evolving nature of your internal world. Recognize that managing anxiety is not a destination but a continual process of adaptation and refinement. The principles explored in this chapter provide a compass, guiding you through the complexities of thought and emotion.

In every thought reframed, in every emotion understood, you cultivate a deeper connection with yourself. The synthesis of cognitive and emotional approaches empowers you to navigate the ebb and flow of anxiety with resilience, creating a narrative of self-discovery and transformation.

Introducing the ABC Model: Deconstructing Thought Patterns

At the core of cognitive restructuring lies the ABC Model—Activating Event, Beliefs, Consequences. Consider it your guiding compass through the labyrinth of your mind. Let's unpack each element, providing you with a roadmap for dissecting and reshaping your thought patterns:

Activating Event: Revealing the Catalyst

The Activating Event acts as the catalyst, the trigger that sets the cognitive wheels in motion. It could be a situation, a fleeting thought, or an external factor initiating the cascade of thoughts leading to anxiety. Envision it as the first note in the symphony of your cognitive processes, the moment that demands your attention and understanding.

Beliefs: Navigating the Lenses of Perception

Delve into the beliefs associated with the Activating Event. These are the lenses through which you perceive the world—your thoughts, interpretations, and perceptions. Unravel the distortions embedded in these beliefs, peeling back the layers to expose the core elements influencing your cognitive landscape.

Consequences: Unmasking the Aftermath

Explore the consequences of your beliefs—the aftermath of the cognitive dance set in motion by the Activating Event. How do these thoughts manifest in your emotions, behaviors, and overall well-being? This exploration provides a clear reflection of the impact, offering insights into the potency of your cognitive patterns.

Step-by-Step Guidance: Crafting Your Cognitive Narrative

Identify the Activating Event: Pinpoint the Catalyst

Start by identifying the triggering event. What happened? What thought or situation initiated the flow of anxious thoughts? Understanding the catalyst is the first step toward gaining control over the narrative of your mind.

Explore Your Beliefs: Delving into Distortions

Dive deep into the beliefs surrounding the Activating Event. What thoughts automatically surfaced? Challenge these beliefs by questioning their accuracy and exploring alternative perspectives, unraveling the distortions that may cloud your cognitive clarity.

Uncover the Consequences: Reflecting on Impact

Examine the consequences of your beliefs. How did they manifest in your emotions, behaviors, and overall well-being? This reflection offers valuable insight into the intricate dance between your thoughts and their real-world effects.

Challenge and Reframe: Transformative Reconstruction

Challenge distorted beliefs by introducing evidence that contradicts them. Is there a more balanced way to view the Activating Event? Reframe your thoughts with a focus on accuracy and resilience, actively participating in the transformative reconstruction of your cognitive narrative.

Case Studies: Beacons of Inspiration

Real-life case studies serve as beacons of inspiration, illustrating the successful application of cognitive restructuring:

Sarah's Journey to Perspective: A Transformative Shift

Sarah, grappling with social anxiety, applied the ABC Model to a networking event. As she identified her Activating Event (entering the room), challenged her beliefs about judgment, and reframed her thoughts, anxiety transformed into a moment of connection. This emotional shift showcases the profound impact of the ABC Model in navigating and reshaping cognitive patterns.

John's Triumph over Catastrophizing: From Anxiety to Empowerment

John, prone to catastrophizing about work projects, navigated the ABC Model. Recognizing the Activating Event, challenging beliefs about failure, and reframing thoughts with a focus on learning, he shifted from anxiety to proactive problem-solving. John's triumph exemplifies the transformative power of the ABC Model, turning moments of distress into opportunities for growth.

Embrace Clarity

As you engage with the ABC Model, remember that it's a dynamic process. Each step contributes to the evolution of your cognitive landscape. By applying this model to anxious thoughts, you become the architect of your cognitive narrative, building a foundation of resilience and clarity that withstands the storms of anxiety.

Mastering Thought Challenges & Reframing

In the realm of cognitive approaches to anxiety, thought challenging and reframing emerge as powerful tools—a dynamic duo designed to unravel the intricacies of negative thoughts and reshape them into beacons of resilience. As we immerse ourselves in this section, envision it as a workshop where you hone the art of challenging and reframing thoughts, sculpting them into allies on your journey toward emotional well-being.

Techniques for Challenging Negative Thoughts:

Negative thoughts often cloak themselves as unassailable truths, weaving a narrative that fuels anxiety. The key is to unveil their distortions and challenge their validity. Here are techniques enriched with context and relatable examples to guide you:

Reality Testing: Uncover the Truth

Act as an objective investigator. Ask yourself, "Is there concrete evidence supporting this thought?" For instance, if your negative belief is about social rejection, consider questioning assumptions and seeking factual evidence from past experiences.

Mindfulness of Thoughts: Clouds in the Sky of Your Mind

Cultivate awareness of your thoughts without immediate judgment. Imagine them as passing clouds in the sky of your mind. This mindful stance allows you to distance yourself from immediate emotional impacts, fostering clarity and a more balanced perspective.

The Evidence Log: Systematic Perspective Accumulation

Create a log where you record evidence supporting or contradicting negative thoughts. For instance, if your negative belief is about your capabilities at work, systematically accumulate instances where you demonstrated competence or received positive feedback.

Guidance on Reframing Thoughts: Crafting a Positive Narrative

Once you've challenged negative thoughts, the next step is to reframe them—transforming their essence into a narrative that fosters positivity and resilience. Here's guidance enriched with examples to illustrate each technique:

Positive Self-Talk: Empowering Affirmations

Introduce positive affirmations and counterstatements to replace negative thoughts. For example, if your negative thought is "I can't handle this," reframe it to "I may face challenges, but I have the strength to navigate them." Visualize a scenario where you successfully navigated a similar challenge.

Exploring Alternative Explanations: Cultivating Curiosity

Encourage curiosity by exploring alternative explanations for the activating event. Consider different perspectives that align with a more balanced and constructive outlook. If your negative belief revolves around personal failures, explore alternative narratives that highlight your growth and achievements.

Best- and Worst-Case Scenarios:

Evaluate the realistic outcomes of the situation. Instead of fixating on catastrophic scenarios, consider a range of possibilities, including more positive and manageable outcomes. Envision scenarios where challenges led to personal growth and resilience.

Before-and-After Scenarios: A Tale of Transformation

Let's delve into before-and-after scenarios to illustrate the profound impact of thought reframing, providing a more nuanced understanding of the emotional consequences:

Before: Catastrophic Thinking

- Negative Thought: "If I make a mistake during the presentation, my career is over."
- Emotional Consequence: Overwhelming anxiety and fear of failure.
- After: Balanced Reframing
- Reframed Thought: "While making mistakes is a part of learning, one presentation does not define my entire career."
- Emotional Outcome: Reduced anxiety and a sense of empowerment to learn from challenges.

Before: All-or-Nothing Thinking

- Negative Thought: "If I can't do this perfectly, it's a complete failure."
- Emotional Consequence: Paralyzing fear and avoidance.
- After: Nuanced Reframing

- Reframed Thought: "Imperfections are a natural part of any endeavor. I can learn and grow from both successes and setbacks."
- Emotional Outcome: Increased resilience and a willingness to embrace the learning process.

As you engage with these techniques, remember that thought challenging and reframing are lifelong skills. Embrace the journey of transformation, knowing that each thought you reshape becomes a stepping stone toward a more resilient and balanced cognitive landscape.

<u>Empowering Solutions: Mastering the Art of Resilient Problem-Solving</u>

In the intricate dance of managing anxiety, problem-solving skills emerge as nimble partners, guiding individuals through the labyrinth of anxiety-inducing situations. This section serves as a comprehensive guide, not just a one-time fix, offering strategies to continuously hone your problem-solving prowess. Practical exercises reinforce these skills, and we explore the transformative impact problem-solving has on alleviating feelings of helplessness and anxiety.

Problem-Solving Strategies: Navigating the Maze

Define the Problem:

Begin by clearly articulating the issue causing distress. Break it down into manageable components to gain a comprehensive understanding.

Brainstorm Solutions:

Engage in a creative process of generating potential solutions. Encourage a free flow of ideas without immediate judgment.

Evaluate Options:

Assess the feasibility, potential outcomes, and consequences of each solution. Consider short-term and long-term implications. Discern which options align with your values and goals.

Make a Decision:

Based on your evaluation, make an informed decision on the most suitable course of action. Trust your judgment and commit to the chosen solution.

Implement the Solution:

Take decisive steps to implement the chosen solution. Break it down into actionable steps, creating a roadmap for execution.

Evaluate the Outcome:

Reflect on the effectiveness of the implemented solution. What worked well? What could be improved? Use this feedback loop for continuous learning.

Exercises to Sharpen Your Problem-Solving Skills

The Problem Diary:

Maintain a problem-solving diary. Document challenges, solutions, and outcomes. Over time, review entries to identify patterns and refine your approach.

Role-Playing Scenarios:

Enlist a trusted friend or family member to engage in role-playing scenarios. Practice applying problem-solving strategies in a simulated environment to build confidence.

Visualizing Success:

Create a visual representation of a successful problem-solving outcome. Whether through drawing, writing, or vision boards, envision the positive resolution of a challenging situation, fostering a sense of accomplishment and boosting problem-solving skills development.

Stories of Empowerment: Problem-Solving in Action

Amy's Workplace Challenge:

Amy faced mounting stress at work due to a challenging project. By applying problem-solving strategies, she identified key priorities, delegated tasks, and sought additional support. Initially overwhelmed, Amy's journey involved emotional turbulence, but through effective problem-solving, she achieved a successful project completion, leading to reduced anxiety and increased self-efficacy.

Mark's Relationship Dynamics:

Struggling with communication issues in his relationship, Mark utilized problem-solving skills to initiate open conversations, actively listen, and collaboratively find solutions. This not only strengthened his relationship but also alleviated anxiety stemming from unresolved issues, showcasing the profound impact of problem-solving on emotional well-being.

Embrace Empowerment

In the journey of anxiety management, the cultivation of problem-solving skills transcends the mere resolution of challenges; it becomes a profound act of self-empowerment. As you engage in the deliberate process of defining, brainstorming, evaluating, deciding, implementing, and evaluating again, you not only address the immediate concerns but also sculpt a resilient mindset.

The iterative nature of problem-solving fosters a continuous learning loop, allowing you to refine your approach and adapt to the dynamic nature of life's challenges.

Furthermore, the empowerment derived from honing problem-solving skills extends beyond the individual. As you navigate the intricacies of your own challenges, you inadvertently contribute to a ripple effect of empowerment within your social circles. By embodying the principles of effective problem-solving, you inspire those around you to approach difficulties with a proactive and constructive mindset. The shared narratives of triumph over adversity become threads in the collective tapestry of empowerment, reinforcing the notion that resilience is not merely a personal endeavor but a communal journey toward strength and self-efficacy.

Cultivating Cognitive Resilience: A Guardian Against Anxiety

Within the intricate landscape of anxiety management, the concept of cognitive resilience unfolds as an artful practice—a shield meticulously crafted to withstand the tempests of anxiety. It involves the cultivation of a robust mental core capable of absorbing the shocks of adversity without succumbing to the torrents of negative thoughts and emotions. Instead of perceiving challenges as insurmountable obstacles, individuals fortified with cognitive resilience view them as opportunities for profound growth and learning.

The Foundations of Cognitive Resilience

Mindful Self-Reflection:

At the heart of cognitive resilience lies mindful self-reflection. In the quiet moments of introspection, you have the opportunity to observe your thoughts and emotions without immediate judgment. This foundational practice enhances self-awareness, providing a sturdy platform upon which resilience can be built. As you delve into the recesses of your mind, you begin to recognize patterns of thought, discerning the triggers that set the stage for anxiety. Mindful self-reflection is akin to preparing the soil before planting seeds—the richer the soil, the more robust the growth.

Affirmations of Strength:

Positive affirmations act as the reinforcing beams of cognitive resilience. When integrated into your daily routine, these affirmations become echoes of strength, reminding you of your capabilities and capacity to overcome challenges. As you repeat these affirmations, they take root in your subconscious, creating a mental infrastructure that withstands the onslaught of self-doubt. Affirmations are not mere words; they are the architecture of resilience, providing the scaffolding that supports you through life's challenges.

Flexible Thinking Exercises:

The mind, much like a muscle, benefits from flexibility exercises. Engaging in activities that promote flexible thinking is akin to stretching the cognitive muscles, enhancing their agility. When faced with challenging situations, individuals with cognitive resilience consciously explore alternative perspectives. This mental gymnastics routine equips them with the capacity to adapt and respond thoughtfully to diverse circumstances. Flexible thinking becomes the secret weapon against the rigidity of anxiety-inducing thoughts.

Gratitude Journaling:

A gratitude journal is the cornerstone of a resilient mindset. Regularly acknowledging and appreciating the positive aspects of your life creates a reservoir of positivity. This practice not only counterbalances anxiety-inducing thoughts but also serves as a wellspring of inspiration during challenging times. The pages of your gratitude journal become a testament to the abundance in your life, reinforcing the narrative of resilience and gratitude.

Mind-Body Connection Practices:

The mind and body are intricately connected, and strengthening this connection is a vital aspect of cognitive resilience. Practices such as yoga, meditation, or deep breathing exercises contribute not only to physical well-being but also foster a harmonious relationship between your thoughts and bodily sensations. These practices become the anchor that grounds you in the present moment, offering a sanctuary of calm amid the storms of anxiety.

Narratives of Triumph: Realizing Cognitive Resilience in Action

Maria's Journey through Uncertainty:

Maria, a dedicated mother and career woman, faced unexpected life changes—divorce and a career shift. Embracing cognitive resilience as her guiding force, Maria reframed these changes as opportunities for personal growth. Daily practices, including mindfulness meditation and flexible thinking exercises, empowered her to adapt to unforeseen circumstances. Maria emerged stronger and more self-assured, a beacon of inspiration illustrating how cognitive resilience transforms uncertainty into a journey of empowerment.

Alex's Triumph Over Catastrophic Thinking:

A young professional battling chronic anxiety, Alex struggled with catastrophic thinking that led to paralyzing fear. Committed to building cognitive resilience, Alex incorporated daily affirmations, challenged negative thought patterns, and engaged in gratitude journaling. Through consistent practice of reframing thoughts and embracing flexibility, Alex not only manages anxiety effectively but has become an advocate for mental health awareness. His triumph over catastrophic thinking stands as a testament to the transformative power of cognitive resilience, inspiring others to believe in their capacity to overcome anxiety and emerge stronger.

The Living Tapestry of Cognitive Resilience

As we navigate the tapestry of cognitive resilience, envision it as a living, breathing entity—one that evolves and adapts to the ebb and flow of life's challenges. The foundations laid through mindful self-reflection, affirmations of strength, flexible thinking exercises, gratitude journaling, and mind-body connection practices contribute to the resilience of this living tapestry.

Mindful Self-Reflection as the Soil:

Imagine mindful self-reflection as the fertile soil that nurtures the roots of cognitive resilience. The introspective moments serve as the bedrock, providing nutrients for the seeds of awareness to sprout and grow. The richer the soil, the deeper the roots penetrate, anchoring the resilience firmly in your psyche.

Affirmations of Strength as Reinforcing Beams:

Affirmations of strength act as the reinforcing beams that support the structure of cognitive resilience. Integrated into your daily routine, these affirmations weave a lattice of positivity and self-belief. With each repetition, the lattice gains strength, becoming a framework that withstands the weight of doubts and uncertainties.

Flexible Thinking Exercises as Cognitive Gymnastics:

Flexible thinking exercises are the cognitive gymnastics routine that keeps the mental muscles agile. Just as gymnasts stretch and contort their bodies to achieve flexibility, engaging in activities that promote flexible thinking ensures that your mind remains supple, ready to adapt to the twists and turns of life.

Gratitude Journaling as the Cornerstone:

The gratitude journal stands as the cornerstone, chronicling the moments of abundance and joy. Its pages are imbued with the colors of positivity, creating a visual narrative of resilience. Each entry reinforces the narrative that, even in challenging times, there is always something to be grateful for.

Mind-Body Connection Practices as the Anchor:

Mind-body connection practices serve as the anchor, grounding the tapestry in the present moment. Like the roots of a tree delving deep into the earth, these practices establish a profound connection between your thoughts and bodily sensations. The anchor provides stability, allowing the tapestry to sway but not be uprooted by the storms.

Embracing Cognitive Resilience as a Transformative Journey

These daily practices and narratives of triumph vividly portray that cognitive resilience is not just a concept but a tangible and transformative journey. Through the prism of Maria and Alex's experiences, we witness the resilience that transcends anxiety, proving that with dedication and belief in one's inner strength, the human spirit can triumph over adversity.

Extending the Tapestry: A Deeper Exploration of Cognitive Resilience

As we extend the exploration of cognitive resilience, delve deeper into the threads that intricately weave this living tapestry. Beyond the foundational practices lie nuanced aspects that enrich the fabric of resilience, contributing to a more intricate and vibrant cognitive landscape.

Narratives of Growth Amidst Challenges:

Within the tapestry of cognitive resilience, individual narratives become threads that weave stories of growth amidst challenges. Imagine these narratives as threads of diverse colors, each representing a unique journey. Some threads may be vibrant and bold, illustrating moments of profound growth, while others may be subtle, portraying the quiet strength found in everyday resilience.

Cognitive Flexibility as the Interwoven Patterns:

Cognitive flexibility, the ability to adapt and shift perspectives, acts as the interwoven patterns that add complexity and depth to the tapestry. Picture these patterns as intricate designs that emerge when the mind embraces change and explores different angles. Cognitive flexibility allows the tapestry to evolve dynamically, mirroring the ever-changing nature of life.

Resilience in the Face of Setbacks:

Resilience in the face of setbacks is the golden thread that runs through the entire tapestry. Envision this golden thread as the luminescent element that illuminates the darkest corners of adversity. It signifies not just bouncing back from challenges but emerging stronger, shining with the brilliance of lessons learned and resilience gained.

The Art of Embracing Uncertainty:

The art of embracing uncertainty is the ethereal thread that adds a touch of mystery to the tapestry. Uncertainty, instead of being feared, becomes an integral part of the design. It symbolizes the unpredictable nature of life and the resilience to navigate the unknown with grace. Embracing uncertainty transforms it from a source of anxiety into a canvas for creative adaptation.

Threads of Wisdom: Navigating the Nuances of Cognitive Resilience

As you navigate the nuances of cognitive resilience, consider these threads of wisdom that guide you through the intricacies of the tapestry. Each thread represents a facet of resilience, offering insights and practices to enhance your cognitive landscape.

Adapting to Change:

In the ever-shifting landscape of life, adaptability becomes a crucial thread. Embrace change not as a disruptor but as a catalyst for growth. Picture this thread as a flexible strand that bends with the winds of change, yet remains unbroken.

Cultivating a Growth Mindset:

Cultivating a growth mindset is the vibrant thread that encourages continuous learning and development. Visualize this thread as a dynamic element that fosters a mindset of curiosity and resilience. A growth mindset perceives challenges not as obstacles but as stepping stones toward personal and emotional growth.

Connection with Others:

The thread of connection with others weaves the fabric of a supportive community. Imagine this thread as a network that intertwines with the threads of individual resilience. Building connections with others strengthens the entire tapestry, creating a collective resilience that weathers storms together.

The Power of Self-Compassion:

Self-compassion is the gentle thread that adds softness to the tapestry. Envision this thread as a soothing balm that nurtures your inner self during challenging times. Practicing self-compassion involves treating yourself with kindness and understanding, acknowledging that imperfections are part of the human experience.

Balancing Optimism and Realism:

The thread of balancing optimism and realism creates a harmonious blend within the tapestry. Picture this thread as a delicate equilibrium between hope and pragmatism. While optimism provides the colors of hope, realism ensures a grounded perspective, fostering resilience that is both aspirational and practical.

Embrace Your Inner Strength

Cognitive resilience is not a finished masterpiece but an ongoing tapestry—a work in progress that evolves with each thought, emotion, and experience. The threads of daily practices, narratives of triumph, and the nuanced exploration of resilience contribute to an unfinished yet beautiful composition.

As you immerse yourself in the journey of cognitive resilience, remember that the tapestry is yours to design. With each mindful reflection, positive affirmation, and flexible thought, you add a thread to the evolving narrative of strength and adaptability. Through stories like Maria's and Alex's, we learn that cognitive resilience is not an endpoint but a continuous journey—an ever-expanding tapestry that holds the potential for boundless growth.

So, as you navigate the intricate landscape of cognitive resilience, consider the threads you weave and the colors you choose. Embrace the unfinished nature of the tapestry, for it is in the continual weaving that the beauty of resilience truly emerges—a vibrant, living testament to the human spirit's capacity to triumph over adversity and embrace the journey toward emotional well-being.

Chapter 4: Behavioral Techniques for Anxiety Reduction

Explore exposure therapy, habit reversal training, exercise benefits, relaxation techniques, and lifestyle changes in this chapter. Uncover exposure therapy principles for a strategic approach to facing anxiety. Experience the transformative process of Habit Reversal Training to break free from anxiety-driven habits. Delve into the neurochemical impact of physical activity with testimonials. Find a melodic refrain in relaxation techniques and consider lifestyle changes as skilled choreographers for overall well-being.

Exposure Therapy Principles: Illuminating the Science of Courage

At the heart of exposure therapy lies a profound understanding—a science of courage that challenges the very essence of fear. Visualize exposure therapy not as a mere confrontation but as a deliberate, strategic engagement with anxiety-provoking situations. It's a transformative journey where individuals systematically face fears, gaining the power to diminish anxiety's grip.

As we delve into the principles of exposure therapy, we peel back the layers of apprehension and uncertainty. Anxiety, much like a shadow, thrives in darkness, and exposure therapy is the light that reveals its true form. This therapeutic approach involves structured exposure—a gradual unfolding of challenges in a safe and supportive environment.

A Guide for Gradual and Safe Self-Exposure: Navigating the Journey

For those ready to embark on the courageous journey of self-exposure, a guide unfolds—one that embraces the delicate dance between challenge and safety. Each step is a deliberate move toward reclaiming power over anxiety, an invitation to face fears at a pace that feels right.

Identify Your Fears:

> Commence by identifying the fears that hold sway over your thoughts. What situations or thoughts trigger anxiety? This clarity is the compass that guides your exposure journey.

Start Small, Progress Gradually:

> The path to resilience is paved with small, intentional steps. Initiate with situations that evoke mild anxiety, allowing yourself to acclimate before moving on to more challenging scenarios. This gradual progression is the key to success.

Create a Safe Space:

Cultivate a safe space for self-exposure—a sanctuary where you can navigate fears without judgment. This might involve enlisting the support of a trusted friend, family member, or mental health professional.

Practice Mindfulness:

Embrace mindfulness as your companion on this journey. Ground yourself in the present moment, acknowledging thoughts and sensations without judgment. Mindfulness serves as the anchor that steadies you amid the waves of anxiety.

Success Stories of Triumph: A Tapestry of Resilience

These are not tales of conquering fear in a single bound but of individuals who, with courage and persistence, faced their anxieties and emerged stronger.

Lisa's Journey from Social Anxiety:

Once paralyzed by social anxiety, Lisa gradually exposed herself to social situations. Starting with small gatherings and working her way up to larger events, Lisa discovered the resilience within her. Today, she not only navigates social interactions with ease but also thrives in environments that once seemed insurmountable. Her emotional transformation paints a vivid picture of the human spirit's capacity to overcome anxiety through exposure therapy.

Tom's Victory Over Phobias:

Plagued by debilitating phobias, Tom embraced exposure therapy to confront his fears head-on. Through gradual exposure to feared objects and situations, Tom dismantled the power these phobias held. His journey is a testament to the transformative potential of facing fears with intention and support. Intention and support become recurring themes in these success stories, reinforcing the idea that exposure therapy is a deliberate and empowering process.

In weaving these success stories, we paint a vivid picture of the human spirit's capacity to overcome anxiety through exposure therapy. These narratives are not meant to be prescriptive but rather inspirational, encouraging readers to embark on their unique journeys toward resilience, armed with the principles and compassion woven into the tapestry of exposure therapy.

Embrace the Courage Within:

Journey into the heart of exposure therapy, where the profound science of courage challenges fear at its core. Imagine this therapeutic approach not as a confrontation but as a strategic engagement with anxiety-provoking situations—a transformative expedition where individuals systematically face fears, reclaiming power over anxiety's grip.

Understanding Habit Reversal Training: A Liberation from Anxiety's Grip

Anxiety, a complex tapestry woven from thoughts and behaviors, often tightens its grip through habitual patterns that provide temporary relief but perpetuate distress. Habit Reversal Training (HRT), grounded in the principles of behavioral therapy, emerges as a beacon of hope—a deliberate and transformative process aimed at dismantling anxiety-driven habits and ushering in healthier alternatives.

Understanding the Web of Anxiety-Driven Habits

Anxiety-related habits are intricate threads in the fabric of an individual's daily life, weaving patterns that, over time, contribute to the entanglement of distress. These habits come in diverse forms—compulsions, rituals, or avoidance behaviors. The first crucial step in HRT is unraveling the complexities of these habits, recognizing them as manifestations of underlying anxiety.

Consider the scenario of Sarah, who grappled with obsessive-compulsive rituals. Her repetitive actions provided momentary relief but intensified the clutches of anxiety. Habit Reversal Training became her guiding light, offering a systematic approach to identify, challenge, and replace these detrimental habits. By acknowledging the compulsions, cultivating awareness, and developing alternative responses, Sarah embarked on a journey of liberation—one where the chains of anxiety-driven habits gradually loosened.

A Strategic Guide to HRT Implementation

Navigating the path of Habit Reversal Training requires a strategic and intentional approach. Each step in the process is a deliberate move toward reclaiming control over habitual responses to anxiety.

1. Identification of the Target Habit:

Begin the journey by pinpointing the specific habit that holds sway over your thoughts and actions. Whether it's a ritual, compulsion, or avoidance behavior, clarity in identification lays the groundwork for subsequent steps.

2. Cultivation of Awareness:

Awareness serves as the compass in the realm of HRT. Understanding when and why the habit manifests is crucial. By shedding light on the triggers and contexts, individuals gain insight into the intricacies of their habitual responses to anxiety.

3. Development of a Competing Response:

Central to HRT is the creation of a competing response—a behavior that runs counter to the identified habit. This intentional shift in behavior serves as a catalyst for breaking free from the chains of anxiety-driven habits. For example, if the habit involves compulsive handwashing, a competing response might involve holding an object with both hands.

4. Rehearsal of the New Response:

Practice becomes the crucible for change. Consistent rehearsal of the competing response in controlled settings gradually introduces a transformative shift. Exposure to situations triggering the habit, coupled with the application of the new response, paves the way for rewiring habitual pathways.

5. Seeking Support and Feedback:

No journey is undertaken in isolation. Enlisting the support of friends, family, or mental health professionals enhances the effectiveness of HRT. Sharing goals, progress, and challenges creates a supportive environment, fostering accountability and encouragement.

Narratives of Liberation: Stories of Triumph Over Anxiety-Driven Habits

The potency of Habit Reversal Training manifests vividly in personal accounts of individuals who have successfully broken free from the chains of anxiety-driven habits.

Sarah's Triumph Over Compulsions:

Sarah's story unfolds as a poignant testament to the transformative power of HRT. Tormented by obsessive-compulsive rituals, Sarah's journey began with the identification of her compulsions. Through meticulous development and consistent application of competing responses, she witnessed a gradual reduction in the grip of her obsessive behaviors. Sarah's triumph stands as a testament to the potential for intentional and targeted change.

Mark's Liberation from Avoidance Behaviors:

Mark, grappling with social anxiety, embarked on a courageous journey of habit reversal to confront his avoidance behaviors. Systematically applying competing responses, Mark not only faced social situations head-on but also discovered newfound empowerment. His story exemplifies the profound impact of breaking free from anxiety-driven habits on emotional well-being.

The Deliberate Process of Habit Reversal: Reshaping Behavioral Patterns

In sharing these personal accounts, we aim to illuminate the deliberate and empowering process of Habit Reversal Training. It is not a quick fix but a transformative journey that reshapes behavioral patterns deeply ingrained by anxiety. As we navigate through the intricacies of this chapter, let these narratives inspire a sense of hope and possibility—an assurance that change is not only achievable but a testament to the resilience of the human spirit in its quest for freedom from anxiety-driven habits.

Expanding the Tapestry: Unveiling the Nuances of Habit Reversal Training

The narrative of Habit Reversal Training extends beyond the surface, delving into the nuances that contribute to its efficacy. Each facet of HRT plays a vital role in the overarching process of liberation from anxiety-driven habits.

1. Contextual Exploration:

An in-depth exploration of the contexts surrounding anxiety-driven habits adds layers to the understanding of their origin. Whether rooted in specific triggers or environmental factors, context provides valuable insights into the intricate dance between habits and anxiety.

2. Integrating Mindfulness:

The incorporation of mindfulness practices enhances the efficacy of HRT. Mindfulness serves as an anchor, grounding individuals in the present moment. As they cultivate awareness without judgment, the habitual responses to anxiety are met with a heightened sense of clarity and intentional action.

3. Addressing Underlying Beliefs:

Habit Reversal Training goes beyond surface-level changes, addressing the underlying beliefs that fuel anxiety-driven habits. By challenging distorted beliefs and fostering cognitive restructuring, individuals embark on a holistic journey toward lasting change.

4. Celebrating Progress:

Acknowledging and celebrating incremental progress is integral to the HRT journey. Each small triumph serves as a building block, reinforcing the newfound habits and creating a positive feedback loop that bolsters resilience against anxiety.

5. Adapting to Evolving Challenges:

An inherent flexibility is woven into the fabric of HRT. Recognizing that challenges evolve, individuals engaged in this process develop adaptive skills. Adjusting and refining the strategies employed in HRT ensure a dynamic and responsive approach to the changing landscape of anxiety.

Personalized Strategies for HRT Success

The success of Habit Reversal Training lies in its adaptability to individual needs. Personalized strategies enhance the effectiveness of HRT, recognizing that each person's journey is unique.

1. Tailoring Competing Responses:

The development of competing responses is not a one-size-fits-all endeavor. Tailoring these responses to align with individual preferences and strengths ensures a more sustainable and personally meaningful approach.

2. Integration of Rewards and Reinforcement:

Incorporating a system of rewards and reinforcement fosters a positive association with the new responses. Celebrating achievements, no matter how small, contributes to the motivational framework that propels individuals forward in their HRT journey.

3. Collaborative Approaches:

Engaging in collaborative approaches, whether through group therapy or involving loved ones in the process, provides a network of support. Shared experiences and collective encouragement create a sense of community, reinforcing the commitment to change.

4. Long-Term Maintenance Strategies:

Habit Reversal Training is not merely a phase but a lifelong skill. Implementing long-term maintenance strategies ensures that the newly acquired habits persist and evolve with the individual's growth. Regular reflection, adjustment of strategies, and continued mindfulness contribute to the enduring success of HRT.

The Transformative Power of Narrative: An Ongoing Tapestry

In unveiling the nuances and personalized strategies of Habit Reversal Training, we contribute to the ongoing narrative of liberation from anxiety-driven habits. The tapestry of HRT is ever-evolving, shaped by the unique experiences and resilience of each individual.

As we delve into the complexities of HRT, let these insights serve as a guide—offering not only a comprehensive understanding of the science behind the approach but also a beacon of hope for those navigating the labyrinth of anxiety-driven habits. The journey of liberation is one of intentional change, and Habit Reversal Training stands as a powerful ally in reshaping the narrative of anxiety into a story of empowerment and resilience.

Habit Reversal Training and Its Interplay with Other Therapeutic Approaches

The journey of overcoming anxiety-driven habits is multifaceted, often requiring a holistic approach that integrates various therapeutic strategies. Habit Reversal Training, while powerful on its own, can synergize with other therapeutic modalities, amplifying its impact on overall well-being.

1. Cognitive-Behavioral Therapy (CBT):

The integration of Habit Reversal Training with Cognitive-Behavioral Therapy (CBT) forms a potent alliance. CBT addresses the cognitive distortions and underlying beliefs contributing to anxiety, complementing the behavioral focus of HRT. The synergy between these approaches provides individuals with a comprehensive toolkit for navigating the complexities of anxiety.

2. Mindfulness-Based Interventions:

Mindfulness practices, with their emphasis on present-moment awareness, seamlessly align with the principles of Habit Reversal Training. The incorporation of mindfulness not only enhances the effectiveness of HRT but also cultivates a deeper understanding of the habitual responses to anxiety. The interplay between mindfulness and HRT creates a harmonious synergy that fosters lasting change.

3. Pharmacological Interventions:

In certain cases, pharmacological interventions may be part of the comprehensive treatment plan. The interplay between Habit Reversal Training and medication is a nuanced dynamic, requiring careful consideration and collaboration between individuals and mental health professionals. The combination of behavioral strategies and pharmacological support can offer a balanced and holistic approach to anxiety management.

Navigating the Integration: A Collaborative Journey to Wellness

The integration of various therapeutic approaches is not a one-size-fits-all endeavor. Navigating this collaborative journey requires a personalized and tailored approach, recognizing the unique needs and preferences of each individual.

1. Collaborative Treatment Planning:

The collaborative integration of therapeutic approaches begins with comprehensive treatment planning. Mental health professionals, in consultation with individuals seeking support, outline a personalized roadmap that draws from the strengths of each therapeutic modality. The shared commitment to the individual's well-being guides the collaborative journey.

2. Flexibility and Adaptability:

Flexibility and adaptability are the cornerstones of integrating therapeutic approaches. Recognizing that individuals may respond differently to various strategies, mental health professionals adjust and tailor the treatment plan based on ongoing feedback and progress. This iterative process ensures a dynamic and responsive approach to individual needs.

3. Open Communication:

Open communication between individuals and mental health professionals is paramount. A transparent dialogue fosters a shared understanding of the therapeutic process, empowering individuals to actively engage in their treatment journey. Regular check-ins and collaborative decision-making contribute to a sense of agency and partnership.

Stories of Integration: A Symphony of Therapeutic Harmony

In exploring the interplay between Habit Reversal Training and other therapeutic approaches, stories of integration emerge as a symphony of therapeutic harmony. These narratives showcase the transformative power of combining strategies to create a comprehensive and tailored approach to anxiety management.

Emily's Journey: A Harmonious Blend of HRT and CBT

Emily, navigating the challenges of generalized anxiety, embarked on a journey that seamlessly integrated Habit Reversal Training and Cognitive-Behavioral Therapy. Recognizing the interplay between her habitual responses to anxiety and distorted thought patterns, Emily worked collaboratively with her therapist to craft a holistic approach. HRT addressed the behavioral manifestations, while CBT provided insights into the cognitive distortions fueling anxiety. The synergy between these approaches empowered Emily to navigate her anxiety with resilience and newfound clarity.

James's Path: Mindfulness, HRT, and Medication in Concert

James, grappling with panic disorder, found solace in an integrated approach that harmonized Mindfulness-Based Interventions, Habit Reversal Training, and pharmacological support. Mindfulness practices anchored James in the present moment, HRT addressed specific anxiety-driven habits, and medication provided a stabilizing foundation. The collaborative efforts of mental health professionals and James himself resulted in a holistic and personalized strategy that transformed his relationship with anxiety.

Embrace the Evolution of Wellness

As we navigate the intricate interplay between Habit Reversal Training and other therapeutic approaches, it becomes evident that the tapestry of wellness is ever-evolving. The integration of strategies contributes to a dynamic narrative—a story of resilience, empowerment, and the ongoing pursuit of well-being.

The Transformative Power of Physical Activity

Physical activity transcends the realms of mere bodily exertion, revealing itself as a dynamic instrument for nurturing mental resilience. It orchestrates a symphony of neurochemical changes, influencing vital messengers such as serotonin and endorphins, which extend their impact beyond the physical to the psychological and emotional dimensions of well-being.

Harmony of Neurotransmitter Regulation:

In the intricate dance of neurochemistry, physical activity emerges as a powerful choreographer. The release of serotonin, often hailed as the "feel-good" neurotransmitter, takes center stage, weaving a sense of calm and well-being into the fabric of the mind. Simultaneously, endorphins, nature's own painkillers, surge through the system, orchestrating a euphoric response that acts as a natural counterbalance to anxiety.

Rhythmic Reduction of Stress Hormones:

The rhythm of exercise becomes a natural stress-reliever, orchestrating a reduction in the production of stress hormones, with cortisol taking a step back. This adept modulation of the body's stress response serves as a soothing melody, mitigating the impact of anxiety-inducing situations and creating a harmonious balance within.

Melodic Improvement of Sleep Patterns:

The melodic tune of regular exercise resonates in the enhancement of sleep quality—an essential note in the composition of anxiety management. As the restorative effects of sleep are amplified, a positive feedback loop is established, contributing harmoniously to the overall symphony of well-being.

Cognitive Crescendo:

Beyond its physical notes, exercise contributes to a cognitive crescendo, fostering enhanced concentration and cognitive flexibility. The symphonic harmonization of these cognitive benefits empowers individuals to navigate the intricate passages of challenges with newfound clarity and resilience.

Weaving Fitness into Life's Symphony:

In the intricate symphony of daily life, the integration of exercise may seem like a complex composition. However, by infusing intentional notes, one can seamlessly weave physical activity into the very fabric of life. These micro-moments of movement, like gentle notes, can be taken during breaks—short walks, stair climbs, or stretching sessions—creating a harmonious rhythm of cumulative physical activity.

Joyful Movements:

Find the joyous melodies in movement. Whether it's the lively dance of joy, the rhythmic pedaling of cycling, or the serene poses of yoga, selecting activities that bring joy adds vibrant hues to the canvas of exercise. Choosing these enjoyable activities not only makes exercise a sustainable part of your routine but transforms it into a harmonious, shared experience.

Social Symphony of Exercise:

Elevate the exercise symphony by infusing a social dimension. Engage in physical activities with friends or family, turning the solo performance into a shared symphony. The harmonious convergence of social connections and physical exertion creates a melodious blend that resonates with joy.

Goals as Musical Crescendos:

Set goals as musical crescendos in the symphony of exercise. Begin with gentle, manageable notes and gradually intensify the composition. These realistic goals, akin to a melodic progression, foster a sense of accomplishment and motivation, creating a harmonious rhythm in your fitness journey.

Testimonials of Transformation Through Exercise:

Within the orchestra of testimonials, Emma's story unfolds as a gentle, serene melody. Grappling with generalized anxiety, she discovered solace in the rhythmic movement of regular walks in nature. This therapeutic ritual significantly reduced her anxiety levels, transforming her evenings into moments of calm—a soothing melody in the symphony of her life.

James, on the other hand, introduces a powerful, empowering chord to the composition. Battling social anxiety, he found strength and confidence in the discipline of strength training. Beyond the physical vigor it bestowed upon him, strength training became a resonant chord that empowered him to confront social situations with newfound assurance a transformative crescendo in his personal symphony.

These testimonials, like musical notes in the grand composition of life, illuminate the diverse ways exercise acts as a catalyst for transformation. From the serene walks embraced by Emma to the empowering strength training experienced by James, exercise unfolds as a personalized journey toward anxiety management—a harmonious tapestry where movement, resilience, and tranquility coalesce. As we immerse ourselves in their narratives, let their stories not only kindle the spark of possibility but resonate as the harmonious acknowledgment that, through movement, we can forge a path to tranquility and resilience.

Embrace the Symphony of Movement

Embark on a profound embrace of the transformative power of physical activity—a symphony that transcends the boundaries of mere exercise and resonates through the corridors of mental resilience. Visualize physical activity as the dynamic conductor orchestrating a complex interplay of neurochemical changes. In this harmonious dance, serotonin and endorphins take center stage, weaving a soothing melody that extends from the physical to the psychological realms.

Relaxation Techniques: Nurturing Serenity in the Midst of Chaos

In the continuation of our symphony for anxiety reduction, we now delve into the realm of relaxation techniques—a melodic refrain that serves as a soothing counterpoint to the discordant notes of stress. Join us on a journey to nurture serenity in the midst of chaos, exploring the art of relaxation through practices such as progressive muscle relaxation and guided imagery.

Teaching Relaxation Techniques:

Progressive Muscle Relaxation (PMR): Unwinding the Tension

The canvas of tranquility is painted with the strokes of Progressive Muscle Relaxation (PMR), a technique that intricately weaves physical and mental relaxation. Picture each muscle group as a note in the symphony of serenity, systematically tensing and then releasing, orchestrating profound harmony within.

Guided PMR Script: A Ballet of Breath and Release

Find a quiet space, close your eyes, and take a deep breath. Inhale, holding tension in your toes for a few seconds, then exhale, releasing the tension. Progressively move upward through your body, each breath orchestrating a dance of relaxation. An accompanying audio resource enhances this experience, allowing a soothing voice to guide you through the symphony of muscle release, creating a tranquil oasis within—a sanctuary where notes of calmness intertwine.

Guided Imagery: Painting Portraits of Calm

Guided Imagery, akin to an artist's brush, entails visualizing peaceful scenes that transport the mind to serene landscapes. Envision a tranquil beach: feel the warmth of the sun, hear the gentle lapping of waves, and breathe in the salty sea air. Engage your senses as you immerse yourself in this tranquil imagery, creating a masterpiece of calmness. Access the provided audio resource for a guided journey, where descriptive narration becomes the brush that paints your mental canvas with scenes of tranquility—an artistic escape into calmness.

Experiences of Relief:

Sarah's Symphony of Calmness: A High-Pressure Overture

Amidst the demands of a high-pressure job, Sarah discovered a personal oasis in progressive muscle relaxation. Through consistent practice, she transformed her evenings into a sanctuary of calmness, unwinding the stress accumulated throughout the day. In the symphony of her life,

PMR became a soothing melody, providing moments of respite and serenity—an overture of calmness in the midst of life's crescendo.

David's Guided Imagery Symphony:

David, navigating the turbulence of anxiety, found refuge in the power of guided imagery. Visualizing serene landscapes became his retreat during anxious moments—a mental escape into a realm of calmness. His experience echoes a harmonious melody that alleviates stress and rejuvenates the spirit—a symphony of escape from life's dissonance.

Embrace Relaxation

These stories, like musical notes in the grand composition of life, illuminate the transformative potential of relaxation techniques. Sarah and David, through their personalized journeys, exemplify how these practices become anchors of tranquility amid life's storms. As we explore the scripts and audio resources, may you find resonance in these experiences, discovering your own oasis of calm within the gentle embrace of relaxation techniques—a harmonious retreat toward serenity.

Lifestyle Changes: Nurturing Balance in the Tapestry of Well-Being

In the intricate choreography of anxiety reduction, lifestyle changes step forward as skilled choreographers, orchestrating a harmonious rhythm that weaves equilibrium into the tapestry of well-being. Immerse yourself in the transformative power of lifestyle adjustments, exploring the realms of sleep, nutrition, and work-life balance.

Embracing Lifestyle Changes: Crafting a Blueprint for Well-being

Sleep Hygiene: Nurturing Restful Nights

Quality sleep stands as the cornerstone of mental well-being, and here we unveil a blueprint for cultivating restful nights.

Bedtime Rituals: A Prelude to Serenity

Engage in a calming pre-sleep routine—a gentle prelude to the symphony of sleep. Activities like reading a book, practicing gentle stretches, or listening to soothing music act as serene notes signaling to your body that it's time to unwind.

Creating a Sleep Haven: Designing Tranquil Spaces

Craft a sleep haven where the ambiance is conducive to rest. Dim the lights, maintain a cool room temperature, and invest in a comfortable mattress and pillows for an optimal sleep sanctuary.

Nutrition: Fueling Mind and Body

A well-nourished body forms the melody of mental resilience, and we explore the harmonious notes of a balanced diet.

Mindful Eating Practices: Savoring the Symphony of Nutrients

Cultivate mindfulness during meals—a mindful symphony of senses. Focus on the sensory experience of eating, savoring each bite, and avoid distractions to enhance the connection between your mind and body.

Hydration: Quenching the Thirst for Balance

Stay adequately hydrated, for dehydration can disrupt the rhythm of mood and cognitive function. Ensure a continuous flow of water throughout the day for a well-hydrated, harmonious body.

Work-Life Balance: Crafting a Fulfilling Sonata

Balancing the professional and personal spheres is a pivotal sonata for mental well-being. Establish boundaries, prioritize self-care, and allocate time for joyous activities to compose a fulfilling narrative.

Setting Boundaries: Defining the Melody of Balance

Delineate work hours and personal time with clarity. Avoid the dissonance of checking work emails or engaging in work-related tasks during designated personal hours.

Joyful Pursuits: Harmonizing Moments of Fulfillment

Dedicate time to activities that bring joy—a harmonizing interlude in the symphony of life. Whether it's reading, communing with nature, or pursuing a hobby, these moments contribute to a resonant sense of fulfillment.

Stories of Transformation: Narratives of Resilience

Emma's Sleep Symphony: Transforming Nights into Sanctuaries

Emma, grappling with insomnia-induced anxiety, orchestrated a sleep revolution. Through consistent bedtime rituals and the creation of a serene sleep environment, she transformed her nights into restful sanctuaries, releasing anxiety's grip in a melodic transformation.

Jake's Nutritional Sonata: A Profound Shift in Harmony

Jake, recognizing the profound link between diet and mood, embarked on a nutritional odyssey. Adopting mindful eating practices and staying hydrated, he experienced a profound shift in mental clarity and emotional balance—a resonant nutritional sonata.

Embrace Your Lifestyle

These stories underscore the profound impact of lifestyle changes. As we traverse the landscapes of sleep, nutrition, and work-life balance, may these narratives inspire you to weave small adjustments into the fabric of your daily life, crafting a symphony of well-being and resilience.

Chapter 5: Emotional Regulation Strategies

In the intricate symphony of anxiety management, the threads of understanding and navigating our emotions weave through the fabric of Chapter 5. This chapter delves into the realm of Emotional Regulation Strategies, guiding readers on a transformative journey to not only identify and acknowledge but also embrace their emotions. Our exploration is not merely about recognizing emotions; it's about cultivating a compassionate relationship with them—a key that unlocks the doors to enhanced anxiety management.

Identifying Emotions: The Language of the Soul

Practical Exercises for Amplifying Emotional Awareness:

Mindful Moments of Reflection:

Embark on intentional moments of self-reflection, focusing on identifying and naming the emotions that dance through the tapestry of your inner world. Naming your emotions becomes a powerful tool for cultivating mindfulness and emotional awareness.

Emotion Journaling:

Uncover the profound benefits of maintaining an emotion journal—a written compass guiding you through the terrain of your emotions. By jotting down feelings and exploring their nuances and triggers, you create a personal roadmap for understanding and navigating your emotional landscape.

Body-Mind Connection:

Recognize the intricate dance of emotions and bodily sensations. Pay keen attention to physical cues—subtle tension in your muscles, comforting warmth, or gentle flutter in your stomach. This awareness forms the foundation of heightened emotional intelligence, fostering a profound understanding of yourself.

Stories of Emotional Awareness Paving the Way for Better Anxiety Management:

In the realm of Emotional Regulation Strategies, stories act as guiding constellations, illuminating the transformative impact of emotional awareness. Let's journey through the narratives of individuals who, like you, navigated the intricate maze of emotions to find solace.

Emma's Discovery of Self-Compassion:

Encounter Emma, initially engulfed by a constant undercurrent of anxiety. Her journey of emotional self-discovery began with the simple yet profound act of identifying and naming her emotions. This practice became her compass, guiding her toward self-compassion. As Emma embraced her feelings without judgment, the grip of anxiety gradually loosened, paving the way for a newfound sense of serenity.

Mark's Path to Emotional Resilience:

Step into Mark's world, where social anxiety presented formidable challenges. Mark recognized the pivotal role of identifying his emotions in the moment. Through acknowledgment without judgment, he not only developed emotional resilience but also found a powerful ally in anxiety management. Mark's story testifies to the liberating power of understanding and accepting one's emotional landscape.

Embrace All Emotions

These stories are not distant examples but companions in your own journey. They illustrate that the path to better anxiety management begins with the recognition and acknowledgment of emotions—an essential foundation for building resilience. As we equip ourselves with the tools to identify and label our emotions, let us extend the invitation to approach them with gentleness and curiosity. In the next section, we will delve into the art of embracing and regulating emotions, offering a compassionate guide for weaving emotional intelligence into the symphony of anxiety management.

Coping with Intense Emotions

In the expansive realm of emotional landscapes, intensity can often resemble a tempest—a potent force that, when skillfully navigated, holds the potential for profound personal growth. This section is a dedicated guide, steering readers through the art of Mastering the Tempest, presenting a versatile toolbox of strategies not only to weather emotional storms but to uncover the transformative potential within them.

Strategies for Navigating Intense Emotional Currents:

Mindful Breathwork:

Embark on the transformative journey of Mindful Breathwork, a practice transcending the mere calming of breath. In moments of emotional intensity, intentional breathwork becomes a cornerstone for fostering emotional resilience. The rhythmic inhales and exhales create a pause, enabling a measured response to the surge of emotions, empowering individuals to navigate intense moments with grace.

Guided Imagery and Visualization:

Delve into the realm of Guided Imagery and Visualization, where imagination becomes a potent tool for emotional regulation. This practice extends beyond creating mental images; it serves as a powerful means of self-soothing. By envisioning serene landscapes or the gradual dissipation of intense emotions, individuals tap into inner reservoirs of calmness.

A Diverse Toolbox of Coping Skills:

Embrace the rich diversity of coping skills as you traverse the intense emotional landscape. Recognizing that each individual's emotional journey is unique, the power of personalization comes to the forefront. Empower yourself with a diverse toolbox of coping skills, acknowledging that the efficacy of each strategy is deeply personal. Experiment, explore, and discover what resonates with your emotional needs and preferences.

Examples of Triumph Over Intense Emotions:
Carlos's Grounding Rituals:

Step into Carlos's world and witness how grounding techniques evolved into transformative rituals for him. By consciously engaging with his senses—touch, sight, and sound—Carlos redirected the energy of intense emotions, preventing them from spiraling out of control. Grounding techniques were not just practices; they became anchors, fundamentally transforming Carlos's emotional state and providing stability amidst the tempest of emotions.

Embrace Resilience

Navigating intense emotions isn't about suppressing or denying them but about cultivating resilience in their presence. In the upcoming section, we will delve into the profound art of embracing and regulating emotions, building upon the foundation of identification and coping established in earlier chapters.

The Art of Self-Compassion

In the intricate tapestry of emotional regulation, one thread radiates with exceptional brilliance—the Art of Self-Compassion. As we navigate through this section, we plunge into the profound significance of cultivating self-compassion in the landscape of anxiety management. Here, we unveil the path to embracing oneself with kindness, offering exercises that serve as stepping stones on the transformative journey toward a more compassionate self-dialogue.

The Crucial Role of Self-Compassion in Confronting Anxiety:

Anxiety, at its core, involves a nuanced interplay of thoughts and emotions, each demanding acknowledgment and understanding. It is within the gentle embrace of self-compassion that individuals discover a sanctuary—a refuge where anxiety can be confronted without self-judgment or criticism. Self-compassion becomes a counterbalance to the often harsh inner critic, providing a balm for the wounds of self-doubt and fear. Emphasize that self-compassion is not about indulgence but about fostering a supportive and understanding relationship with oneself.

Mindful Self-Compassion Meditation:

Embark on the transformative journey of Mindful Self-Compassion Meditation with a concise overview of its steps. This guided meditation seamlessly integrates mindfulness and self-compassion, encouraging readers to observe their thoughts and emotions without judgment. The meditation consciously cultivates an attitude of warmth and understanding toward oneself, providing a structured practice for fostering self-compassion.

Personal Narratives of Transformation Through Self-Compassion:

Explore the profound power of self-compassion through authentic life stories, each serving as a guiding light toward the transformative realm of self-compassion.

Emma's Voyage to Self-Love:

Embark on Emma's transformative journey through self-compassion, where the tenacious grip of anxiety encounters the soothing balm of kindness. By consciously challenging her self-critical thoughts and replacing them with words of compassion, Emma discovers a newfound sense of self-love. Emma's narrative vividly illustrates the profound impact of self-compassion in rewriting the narrative of anxiety.

Alex's Unearthing of Inner Strength:

> Step into Alex's world and grasp how embracing a compassionate stance contributes to his unearthing of inner strength. Confronting tumultuous waves of panic attacks, Alex not only weathers the storms of anxiety but emerges with resilience. Alex's narrative showcases the liberating power of self-compassion, transforming vulnerability into a source of strength.

Embrace You

As we progress in our exploration of emotional regulation strategies, may the practices and stories shared in this section serve as lanterns, illuminating the path to a gentler, more compassionate relationship with oneself amid the challenges of anxiety.

Communicating Your Emotions Effectively

Effective communication stands as an art form, especially when articulating the complexities of our emotions. Within the realm of anxiety management, mastering mindful expression in conversation becomes a cornerstone for fostering understanding and connection. Here, we delve into nuanced communication techniques that transcend spoken words, creating a space where emotions can be shared with openness and empathy.

Active Listening as a Pillar of Mindful Expression:

In the symphony of communication, active listening plays a crucial role. It involves not just hearing the words spoken but truly comprehending their essence. As individuals navigate the intricacies of anxiety, being actively heard can be profoundly validating. Encouraging loved ones to express their thoughts and emotions without interruption fosters an environment where anxiety can be explored with depth and sincerity.

Empathetic Reflection:

Empathy forms the bedrock of understanding, and incorporating empathetic reflection into conversations elevates the quality of communication. This technique involves mirroring the emotions expressed by a loved one, demonstrating that their feelings are acknowledged and understood. For instance, responding with phrases like "It sounds like you're feeling..." or "I can imagine that must be tough..." creates a bridge of empathy, fortifying the connection and providing a sense of shared emotional space.

Non-Verbal Cues:

Words only scratch the surface of communication; non-verbal cues often carry profound meaning. Encouraging individuals to pay attention to non-verbal expressions, such as body language and facial expressions, enhances the depth of connection. It's the subtle nuances—the furrowed brow, the gentle nod, or the comforting touch—that contribute to a richer understanding of emotions beyond the spoken language.

Mindful Presence:

Amidst the whirlwind of anxiety, cultivating mindful presence during conversations becomes transformative. This involves being fully engaged in the moment, setting aside distractions, and offering undivided attention. Mindful presence communicates not just words but a genuine commitment to understanding and supporting a loved one through their emotional journey.

Validation Techniques:

Validating someone's emotions is a powerful affirmation of their experience. Techniques such as paraphrasing or summarizing the expressed emotions demonstrate that their feelings are heard and acknowledged. Using phrases like "It makes sense that you would feel..." or "I hear you saying that..." conveys validation, creating a safe space for open dialogue.

Fostering a Collaborative Environment:

Anxiety can be a shared experience, and approaching conversations with a collaborative mindset strengthens connections. Encouraging loved ones to express their perspectives on anxiety and co-create solutions fosters a sense of partnership. Framing discussions as collaborative endeavors, rather than one-sided interactions, empowers individuals to actively contribute to their anxiety management strategies.

Cultivating Emotional Intelligence:

Emotional intelligence involves understanding and managing one's emotions and empathizing with the emotions of others. Encouraging the development of emotional intelligence through reflective conversations and exploring the emotional landscape together deepens connections. This self-awareness and empathy lay the groundwork for constructive and supportive communication.

Real-Life Stories of Transformative Communication:

Sarah and Michael's Dialogical Dance:

Sarah and Michael, a couple navigating anxiety, discovered the power of dialogical communication. Through active listening, empathetic reflection, and validation, they created a space where both felt seen and understood. This dialogical dance not only strengthened their bond but became a model for navigating anxiety collaboratively.

Parent-Child Connection:

In a family dynamic, effective communication is paramount. A parent, upon learning about their child's anxiety, employed active listening and validation techniques. This not only enhanced the parent-child relationship but also empowered the child to express their emotions openly, fostering a sense of security.

Workplace Support:

In professional settings, communication about anxiety can be delicate. An employee, experiencing anxiety, found solace in a manager who embraced mindful expression. By fostering a collaborative environment and offering empathetic support, the manager not only contributed to the employee's well-being but also cultivated a workplace culture of understanding.

Embrace Your Voice

Navigating anxiety through communication is an intricate dance—one where words, empathy, and understanding converge. These communication techniques serve as instruments for crafting meaningful connections and nurturing emotional well-being. As individuals incorporate these techniques into their interactions, may they find solace in the transformative power of mindful expression, fostering connections that withstand the tempests of anxiety.

Safeguarding Emotional Well-being

In the intricate composition of emotional well-being, safeguarding against emotional burnout emerges as a crucial thread—a fundamental aspect of self-care that empowers individuals to navigate life's challenges with resilience and grace. This section serves as a gentle guide, offering strategies for preventing burnout, insights into recognizing early signs, and narratives of recovery to inspire those standing on the brink of emotional exhaustion.

Strategies for Proactive Well-being:

Setting Firm Boundaries:

The cornerstone of preventing burnout rests on the establishment and preservation of healthy boundaries. Acknowledging personal limits and effectively communicating them ensures a sustainable approach to managing life's demands. Setting boundaries is not a sign of weakness but a proactive step toward preserving one's emotional equilibrium.

Elevating Self-Care Priorities:

Self-care transforms from a luxury to a necessity. This exploration delves into practical self-care routines designed to replenish emotional reserves, fostering a continuous sense of well-being even in the face of life's persistent stressors. Prioritizing self-care becomes an act of self-empowerment, nurturing a foundation for emotional resilience.

Harnessing Mindfulness Practices:

Mindfulness emerges as an anchor, grounding individuals in the present moment. Techniques like meditation and mindful breathing become invaluable tools in the prevention of emotional burnout, fostering overall mental wellness. Mindfulness is not merely a practice but a way of infusing intention and awareness into every facet of life.

Recognizing Early Signs:

Cognitive and Emotional Exhaustion:

Early detection of cognitive and emotional exhaustion stands as the primary defense against burnout. This exploration delves into the subtle signs that serve as red flags, indicating when it's time to pause, reflect, and prioritize self-nurturing. Awareness of one's mental and emotional state becomes a compass for navigating the complexities of well-being.

Sleep and Energy Pattern Awareness:

Disruptions in sleep and energy levels often precede burnout. Understanding these shifts provides valuable insights into one's emotional well-being and acts as an early warning system for potential burnout. Sleep and energy become barometers for gauging emotional resilience.

Embracing Emotional Resilience Shifts:

Emotional resilience undergoes transformations in the face of burnout. Exploring these shifts builds awareness, empowering individuals to intervene with self-compassion and preventive measures. Recognizing and embracing emotional changes become integral components of the proactive strategy against burnout.

Stories of Recovery to Ignite Resilience:

Jason's Odyssey from Burnout to Balance:

Jason's narrative echoes the universal struggle with burnout. Through a profound journey of self-discovery and the implementation of preventative strategies, Jason not only rebounded from burnout but also crafted a life that prioritizes well-being. His story serves as a testament to the transformative power of resilience.

Ella's Endurance in the Face of Exhaustion:

Ella's tale stands as a testament to the resilience of the human spirit. By recognizing early signs of burnout, implementing self-care practices, and seeking support, Ella emerged from the depths of emotional exhaustion with newfound strength. Her journey inspires a profound sense of endurance and the possibility of renewal.

Embrace Sustainability

As you navigate the nuances of preventing and recovering from emotional burnout, may these strategies and stories become guiding lights, illuminating the path towards a life that is not only productive but deeply nourishing to the soul. The tapestry of emotional well-being continues to unfold, with each thread interweaving to create a robust foundation. In the upcoming section or chapter, we will seamlessly transition into new dimensions of understanding and practices that enrich the intricate landscape of anxiety management.

Chapter 6: Using Technology to Manage Anxiety

In the dynamic landscape of anxiety management, technology emerges as a transformative force, ushering in new avenues for support and empowerment. This chapter delves into the realm of harnessing technology to alleviate anxiety, with a specific focus on Mobile Apps for Anxiety Management. As we navigate the diverse applications available, our goal is not merely to introduce tools but to guide readers in seamlessly incorporating them into their personalized anxiety management strategies.

Mobile Apps for Anxiety Management

In the swift currents of our daily lives, mobile apps have evolved beyond mere communication tools; they are now gateways to well-being. A plethora of apps is meticulously designed to address anxiety management, equipping users with resources and strategies to cultivate mental resilience.

Calm: A Tranquil Sanctuary

> Calm stands out as a comprehensive app, presenting users with guided meditations, soothing sounds, and sleep stories. Its user-friendly interface and diverse content make it a sanctuary for those seeking moments of tranquility amidst the hustle of daily life.

Headspace: Making Meditation Accessible

> Headspace demystifies meditation, deconstructing it into bite-sized sessions suitable for both beginners and seasoned practitioners. With its vibrant animations and structured programs, Headspace serves as a virtual meditation companion, fostering mindfulness within even the busiest schedules.

Wysa: Your AI Mental Health Companion

> Wysa takes a distinctive approach by integrating artificial intelligence. This chatbot-based app provides users with a confidential space to express their thoughts and feelings, offering evidence-based therapeutic techniques to manage anxiety in real-time.

Weaving Apps into Your Anxiety Management Symphony:

While these apps offer valuable resources, their integration into a holistic anxiety management strategy enhances their effectiveness. Consider the following tips:

- Consistency is Key: Weave app usage into your daily routine. Whether it's a morning meditation or an evening wind-down with sleep stories, consistency fosters habit and maximizes benefits.
- Pair with Other Strategies: Combine app usage with other anxiety management strategies like exercise, mindfulness, or journaling. The synergy of multiple approaches contributes to a more robust well-being plan.
- Personalization Matters: Explore different apps to find what resonates with you. Each person is unique, and the effectiveness of these tools often depends on personal preferences and individual needs.

User Voices:

Real-world experiences provide valuable insights into the impact of these apps. Let's hear from individuals who have found solace and support:

Emma's Journey with Calm:

- "Calm has become my sanctuary. The guided meditations help me find peace amid chaos. It's not just an app; it's a companion in my journey to manage anxiety."

James' Headspace Experience:

- "Headspace made meditation accessible for me. The animations are engaging, and the sessions are just the right length. It's like having a meditation coach in my pocket."

Amanda's Reflection on Wysa:

- "Wysa feels like a personal mental health companion. The AI aspect is intriguing, and the techniques suggested have been surprisingly effective in moments of anxiety."

Embrace Digital Tools:

As we embark on the exploration of mobile apps for anxiety management, may this digital journey empower you to embrace the tools that resonate with your unique path. In the upcoming sections, our exploration of technology's role in anxiety management will unfold, shifting the focus to the realm of online therapy and support.

Navigating the Virtual Landscape: Online Therapy and Support

Revealing the Advantages:

Access Beyond Borders:

Online therapy dismantles geographical constraints, providing individuals with the opportunity to connect with licensed therapists, irrespective of their location. This newfound accessibility is a transformative element, particularly beneficial for those residing in remote areas or facing mobility challenges.

Comfort in Your Sanctuary:

The therapeutic setting extends to the comfort of one's own space. Online sessions offer a unique intimacy, enabling individuals to partake in therapy from the familiar environment of their homes. This setting enhances feelings of safety and openness during the therapeutic process.

Adaptable Scheduling for Modern Lifestyles:

In a world characterized by dynamic schedules, online therapy proves flexible. With adaptable scheduling options, individuals can seamlessly integrate therapy into their lives without the confines of traditional office hours.

Considerations on the Virtual Front:

Technological Challenges:

While technology opens doors, it also poses challenges. Stable internet connectivity and familiarity with video conferencing tools are critical factors. Addressing and acknowledging these challenges ensures a smoother and more effective therapeutic experience.

Privacy and Confidentiality:

Upholding the confidentiality of online therapy is of utmost importance. Before embarking on this journey, individuals should choose a secure and reputable platform that prioritizes privacy. Openly discussing confidentiality measures with the selected therapist is also encouraged.

Tailoring the Approach:

Recognizing that online therapy may not suit everyone is essential. It's crucial to assess personal preferences and needs. While some individuals thrive in face-to-face interactions, others find the virtual setting conducive to self-reflection.

Discovering Credible Online Therapy Services:

Navigating the myriad of online therapy options demands a discerning eye. Here's a guide:

Research and Reviews:

Delve into reputable online therapy platforms through reviews and testimonials. Platforms with positive feedback and licensed professionals are more likely to provide a reliable therapeutic experience.

Credentials and Licensing:

Verify that therapists on the chosen platform hold proper licensing and accreditation. This ensures adherence to ethical standards and confirms their qualifications to offer effective support.

Free Consultations:

Many online therapy platforms offer complimentary consultations. Utilize these opportunities to assess the therapist's approach, ensuring it aligns with your needs and comfort.

Testimonials: Narratives of Breakthroughs

Real-life stories illuminate the transformative power of online therapy:

Sarah's Liberation from Social Anxiety:

"Online therapy offered a secure space to confront my social anxiety. The virtual setting allowed me to take gradual steps, and my therapist's support empowered me to navigate social situations with newfound confidence."

David's Journey to Self-Discovery:

"Connecting with a therapist online felt less intimidating. It was liberating to explore my thoughts and feelings in the comfort of my home. Online therapy became a catalyst for my journey to self-discovery."

Embrace Confidence:

May this glimpse into the world of online therapy instill confidence in the potential of virtual support. In the subsequent sections, we will continue our exploration, shifting our focus to the realm of mobile apps designed to complement anxiety management strategies.

Unleashing the Potential of Biofeedback:

Decoding the Essence of Biofeedback:

Biofeedback is a transformative process enabling individuals to cultivate awareness and command over physiological functions through electronic monitoring. Serving as a conduit between the mind and body, this tool provides real-time feedback on various physiological markers, such as heart rate, muscle tension, and skin temperature.

The Mechanics of Biofeedback:

Engaging in biofeedback sessions involves attaching sensors to different parts of the body. These sensors detect physiological changes, presenting the feedback visually or auditorily. Through consistent sessions, individuals learn to consciously influence these physiological responses, fostering a profound sense of control over their bodily reactions to stress and anxiety.

Advantages of Biofeedback:

Elevated Self-Awareness:

> Biofeedback enriches self-awareness by offering tangible data on bodily responses to stress.

Precision in Stress Reduction:

> Empowered with specific information, individuals can employ targeted techniques to alleviate stress and anxiety.

Tailored Interventions:

> Biofeedback facilitates the creation of personalized interventions, aligning with an individual's unique physiological patterns.

Wearable Technology: Your Ally in Anxiety Management

Unveiling the World of Wearable Technology:

Wearable devices, ranging from smartwatches to fitness trackers, have seamlessly integrated into our daily lives. In the realm of anxiety management, these devices serve as invaluable companions, providing continuous monitoring and real-time data insights.

Harnessing the Power of Wearable Technology:

Equipped with sensors, wearable devices can track key physiological indicators associated with anxiety, including heart rate variability, sleep patterns, and physical activity levels. This real-time data empowers individuals to recognize patterns, identify triggers, and implement timely interventions.

Benefits of Wearable Technology:

Continuous Monitoring:

> Wearable devices deliver ongoing monitoring, offering a comprehensive view of one's well-being.

Timely Intervention:

> Real-time data alerts individuals to changes in physiological markers, enabling proactive and targeted interventions.

Integration into Daily Life:

> Wearable technology seamlessly integrates into daily routines, fostering consistent anxiety management practices.

Case Studies: Narratives of Triumph through Technology

Emily's Journey to Heart Rate Coherence:

"Biofeedback became my guiding light in navigating anxiety. Mastering heart rate coherence through biofeedback sessions empowered me to regulate my emotions in real-life situations. It's akin to having a personal guide for my mental well-being."

Jason's Insights from Wearable Tech:

"Wearable technology opened my eyes to the correlation between my sleep patterns and anxiety levels. Armed with this awareness, I implemented lifestyle changes and witnessed a profound improvement in my overall mental health. It's akin to having a health coach on my wrist."

Embrace Technological Allies:

As we immerse ourselves in the realm of Biofeedback and Wearable Technology, let these insights kindle a newfound appreciation for the ways in which technology can become a potent ally in our journey toward anxiety management. In the forthcoming sections, our exploration will continue, shifting our focus to the integration of mobile apps designed to complement and enhance these innovative tools.

Navigating Anxiety through Virtual Reality

Embarking on the Virtual Journey:

Virtual Reality Exposure therapy immerses individuals in simulated environments to safely confront and navigate anxiety-provoking situations. By harnessing the power of technology, VR provides a controlled and customizable space for exposure, unlocking new therapeutic avenues.

The Transformative Potential of VR in Anxiety Management:

Immersive Exposure:

> VR empowers individuals to confront anxiety triggers in a controlled and immersive setting, facilitating a gradual and guided exposure experience.

Customizable Scenarios:

> Therapists can tailor virtual scenarios to align with specific anxiety triggers, ensuring personalized and targeted exposure sessions.

Safe and Controlled Environment:

> VR establishes a secure space for individuals to confront fears, fostering a sense of empowerment and mastery over anxiety-inducing situations.

Limitations and Considerations:

While VR holds immense potential in anxiety management, acknowledging its limitations is crucial. Factors like the cost of equipment, accessibility, and potential discomfort during virtual exposure should be considered. It's also important to recognize that individuals may respond differently to this form of therapy.

Triumphant Narratives in the Virtual Realm:

Sarah's Transformation through VR Exposure:

"Virtual Reality Exposure therapy unlocked a door to confront my social anxiety. In the virtual realm, I could gradually expose myself to social scenarios, building confidence at my own pace. It's a game-changer that turned my anxiety into a conquerable challenge."

David's Journey to Overcoming Phobias:

"As someone grappling with specific phobias, VR exposure therapy offered a bespoke solution. Confronting my fears in a virtual setting allowed me to build resilience and eventually face these fears in real life. It's like having a virtual bridge to a phobia-free reality."

Embrace Information

In the digital age, information is a powerful ally in our quest for mental well-being. This section of the chapter delves into the pivotal role of staying informed about anxiety—how knowledge becomes a beacon of empowerment, guiding individuals through the intricate landscape of their mental health. As we continue our exploration, the subsequent sections will unfold, shedding light on other technological tools that enhance and complement our journey towards well-being.

The Empowering Essence of Knowledge

Unveiling the Impact of Information:

In the pursuit of anxiety management, understanding the intricacies of anxiety is akin to wielding a compass. Knowledge grants us the ability to decipher the language of our emotions, recognize triggers, and chart a course toward effective coping strategies. By staying informed, individuals can demystify anxiety, transforming it from an enigmatic force into a challenge with tangible solutions.

Resources for Credible Information:

The digital realm offers a vast array of resources, and discerning credible sources is crucial. Online platforms, reputable mental health websites, and apps curated by professionals provide valuable insights into anxiety disorders, coping mechanisms, and the latest advancements in mental health research. These resources serve as digital companions, offering guidance at one's fingertips.

Knowledge as a Pillar of Empowerment:

Understanding anxiety on a deeper level is an empowering journey. Individuals armed with knowledge not only gain insight into their own mental health but also become advocates for breaking the stigma surrounding anxiety. As we unravel the complexities of anxiety through information, we empower ourselves and others to navigate this terrain with resilience and understanding.

Stories of Knowledge Empowering Anxiety Management:

Mia's Journey to Self-Understanding:

"Knowledge became my anchor in the storm of anxiety. Learning about different anxiety disorders, their manifestations, and coping strategies transformed my perspective. I no longer felt lost; I felt equipped to navigate the challenges that anxiety presented."

Aiden's Advocacy through Information:

"Being informed about anxiety didn't just help me manage my struggles but turned me into an advocate. Sharing reliable information on mental health, both online and offline, became my way of contributing to a community that needed understanding and support."

Embrace Your Knowledge

As we embark on the exploration of using technology to manage anxiety, let us recognize the invaluable role that staying informed plays in this journey. In the forthcoming sections, we will delve into specific technological tools and resources that harness the power of information for enhanced mental well-being.

Chapter 7: Alternative and Complementary Therapies

Explore a variety of alternative and complementary therapies, from natural remedies to ancient practices, all aimed at fostering mind-body harmony for comprehensive anxiety relief. The chapter underscores the significance of considering diverse strategies, providing a nuanced understanding of alternative therapeutic options.

Nourishing Nature's Remedies:

In the expansive realm of anxiety management, this chapter's first section delves into the intriguing landscape of Herbal and Nutritional Supplements. These complementary therapies, derived from nature's bounty, offer a unique avenue for individuals seeking holistic approaches to alleviate anxiety symptoms.

Understanding the Role of Supplements:

Herbs and nutritional supplements have been woven into the tapestry of traditional medicine for centuries, revered for their potential to promote mental well-being. In this section, we explore the ways in which these supplements can play a role in managing anxiety. From herbal infusions to carefully crafted nutritional blends, nature provides a diverse palette to support our mental health.

Research Insights into Various Supplements:

An evidence-based approach is crucial when considering herbal and nutritional supplements. We'll embark on a journey through current research, shedding light on the effectiveness of specific supplements in alleviating anxiety symptoms. Understanding the science behind these natural remedies empowers individuals to make informed decisions about incorporating them into their wellness routine.

Guidelines for Safe and Informed Use:

While nature's remedies hold promise, it is essential to navigate this terrain with caution. This section offers practical guidelines for the safe use of herbal and nutritional supplements. From dosage recommendations to potential interactions with medications, these guidelines aim to empower individuals to make choices that align with their overall health and well-being.

Stories of Natural Support:

Sophie's Herbal Infusion Ritual:

"Incorporating herbal infusions into my daily routine became a ritual of self-care. The calming effects of chamomile and lavender not only eased my anxious thoughts but also created a serene moment of respite amidst life's chaos."

Research-Informed Choices for Carlos:

"Reading about the research on nutritional supplements gave me the confidence to explore natural options. Discussing these choices with my healthcare provider ensured a holistic approach to managing my anxiety, combining conventional and complementary therapies."

Embrace the Wisdom Nature Offers:

As we navigate the realm of alternative and complementary therapies, let us embrace the wisdom nature offers. The journey through herbal and nutritional supplements becomes not just a path to anxiety management but a holistic exploration of our body's connection to the healing forces of the natural world. In the upcoming sections, we will continue to unravel diverse avenues for complementing traditional approaches to anxiety.

Navigating Ancient Practices

Introduction to Acupuncture:

Acupuncture, a cornerstone of traditional Chinese medicine, has garnered attention for its potential in treating various health conditions, including anxiety. In this section, we explore the principles of acupuncture—where thin needles are strategically inserted into specific points on the body—to restore the flow of vital energy, known as Qi. As we delve into this time-honored practice, we unravel its potential role in anxiety management.

Traditional Medicine Practices:

Beyond acupuncture, various traditional medicine practices from cultures around the world contribute to the rich tapestry of alternative therapies. From Ayurveda to Indigenous healing traditions, this section provides an overview of these practices and their holistic approach to addressing the interconnectedness of mind, body, and spirit in anxiety management.

The Tapestry of Evidence:

Research Supporting Acupuncture and Traditional Medicine:

While rooted in ancient wisdom, these practices are not immune to scrutiny. We explore contemporary research supporting the efficacy of acupuncture and traditional medicine in managing anxiety. Understanding the evidence allows individuals to make informed decisions about incorporating these alternative therapies into their anxiety management toolkit.

Personal Stories of Healing:

Emma's Acupuncture Journey:

"Acupuncture became a sanctuary for me. The gentle insertion of needles and the subsequent sense of balance and calmness transformed my relationship with anxiety. It was more than a physical experience; it was a journey inward, reconnecting with the essence of well-being."

Carlos's Exploration of Traditional Healing:

"Exploring traditional medicine practices rooted in my cultural heritage was a revelation. The holistic approach, integrating physical, mental, and spiritual elements, provided a profound sense of grounding. It was more than symptom relief; it was a journey of self-discovery and connection."

Embracing Holistic Alternatives:

As we explore the realms of acupuncture and traditional medicine, let us embrace the wisdom encapsulated in these time-tested practices. The journey through alternative and complementary therapies becomes a celebration of diverse approaches to anxiety management, acknowledging that healing is a tapestry woven from various threads. In the subsequent sections, we will continue to unravel the rich fabric of alternative therapies, offering a comprehensive guide for individuals seeking holistic paths to well-being. In the tapestry of alternative and complementary therapies, Section 1 of this chapter invites you to embark on a journey into the profound realms of Mindfulness and Meditation. These ancient practices, deeply rooted in contemplative traditions, offer a sanctuary for the mind amidst the challenges of anxiety.

Cultivating Mindfulness

Exploring Mindfulness Practices:

Mindfulness, the art of being fully present in the current moment, is a beacon of tranquility in the storm of anxiety. In this section, we delve into mindfulness practices, ranging from mindful breathing to body scan meditations. These practices cultivate an awareness that transcends the chaotic landscape of anxious thoughts.

Guided Meditation Exercises:

Embark on a journey of self-discovery with guided meditation exercises. From grounding meditations that anchor you in the present to loving-kindness meditations that foster compassion, each exercise is a step towards cultivating a mindful presence. Practical and accessible, these exercises become tools in your anxiety management toolkit.

Guidance for Meditation Novices:

For those new to meditation, this section offers gentle guidance on starting the journey. Understand the simplicity and power of mindfulness, demystifying any misconceptions that may hinder your initial steps into the world of meditation.

Recommended Resources:

Explore a curated list of resources, including meditation apps, guided recordings, and written materials, to support your mindfulness journey. These resources act as companions, providing guidance and structure as you navigate the vast landscape of meditation.

Stories of Profound Transformation:

Emma's Path to Inner Calm:

"Mindfulness became my sanctuary. In the midst of anxiety's turbulence, I found a refuge in the simple act of breathing. Each mindful breath became a tether to the present, gradually quieting the storm within."

Mark's Discovery of Peace:

"Meditation was my anchor in the sea of anxiety. As I delved into the practice, I discovered an oasis of calm within. It wasn't about silencing the mind; it was about befriending its fluctuations and finding peace amidst the chaos."

Embracing the Present Moment:

As we explore the realms of mindfulness and meditation, let us embrace the transformative power encapsulated in the present moment. The journey into these contemplative practices becomes an odyssey of self-discovery and peace, offering solace amidst the challenges of anxiety. In the subsequent sections, we will continue to unravel the diverse threads of alternative therapies, providing a comprehensive guide for those seeking holistic paths to well-being.

Yoga and Tai Chi – A Harmony of Body and Mind

In the symphony of alternative and complementary therapies, we now venture into the graceful realms of Yoga and Tai Chi. These ancient practices, revered for their holistic benefits, offer a serene pathway towards managing anxiety and nurturing mental well-being.

The Healing Power of Yoga:

Benefits for Anxiety Management:

Yoga, with its union of breath, movement, and mindfulness, emerges as a gentle yet potent ally in the quest for anxiety relief. Delve into the transformative effects of yoga on the nervous system, fostering a sense of calm and balance. From grounding poses to soothing breathwork, each aspect of yoga contributes to creating harmony within.

The practice of yoga is an exploration of self-discovery and inner connection. By synchronizing breath with movement, individuals engage in a meditative flow that transcends the physical postures. This mindful approach not only promotes flexibility in the body but also encourages flexibility in the mind, allowing practitioners to navigate the uncertainties of life with greater ease.

Starting Your Yoga Journey:

For those stepping onto the yoga mat for the first time, this section provides practical tips and guidance. Discover beginner-friendly poses and sequences designed to ease you into the practice, allowing you to gradually unlock the benefits of yoga for anxiety management.

Embarking on a yoga journey is a personal odyssey, and it begins with finding comfort on the mat. Starting with foundational poses and gentle stretches, beginners can cultivate a sense of body awareness and mindfulness. The emphasis is not on perfection but on the exploration of one's own capabilities and limitations, fostering a nurturing environment for self-discovery.

Beyond the physical postures, the breath is a central element in yoga practice. Learning to synchronize breath with movement enhances the mind-body connection, promoting a state of focused awareness. This meditative aspect of yoga becomes a valuable tool for managing anxiety, as individuals learn to anchor themselves in the present moment and let go of intrusive thoughts.

The Graceful Dance of Tai Chi:

Mindful Movement for Mental Well-being:

Tai Chi, often referred to as a moving meditation, invites practitioners into a dance of slow, deliberate movements. Explore how the rhythmic flow of Tai Chi harmonizes breath, body, and mind, creating a tranquil space that counters the turbulence of anxiety. Tai Chi becomes a moving meditation, offering profound mental and physical benefits.

The ancient Chinese practice of Tai Chi is a dance of serenity that unfolds through deliberate, flowing movements. Each posture is executed with a focus on internal energy flow, promoting a sense of balance and harmony. The slow and intentional nature of Tai Chi encourages individuals to be fully present in the movements, fostering a state of mindfulness that transcends the anxieties of daily life.

Embarking on Tai Chi:

This section welcomes beginners to the art of Tai Chi, offering insights into its principles and providing simple exercises to initiate your practice. Tai Chi's emphasis on flowing movements and mindful awareness makes it accessible to individuals of all fitness levels.

Embarking on the journey of Tai Chi is an exploration of the body's innate wisdom and the art of moving meditation. Beginners can start with basic Tai Chi forms that focus on cultivating a sense of balance, coordination, and tranquility. The gentle, rhythmic motions become a moving meditation, allowing individuals to connect with their breath and the present moment.

The philosophy behind Tai Chi aligns with the principles of traditional Chinese medicine, viewing the body and mind as interconnected aspects of a unified whole. By engaging in the graceful movements of Tai Chi, individuals not only enhance their physical well-being but also cultivate mental resilience and inner calm.

Narratives of Transformation:

Sarah's Journey to Serenity through Yoga:

"Yoga became my sanctuary amidst the chaos of anxiety. Each pose was a mindful step towards grounding, and with each breath, I reclaimed a sense of control. Yoga wasn't just about flexibility; it was about finding flexibility in my mind amidst life's uncertainties."

Sarah's experience highlights the transformative power of yoga as a sanctuary for the mind. Through the practice of yoga, she discovered a profound sense of grounding and control amid the chaos of anxiety. The intentional movements and breathwork became a therapeutic journey, allowing her to navigate life's uncertainties with newfound flexibility and resilience.

Alex's Tai Chi Discovery:

"The rhythmic flow of Tai Chi became a dance of peace for me. In its gentle movements, I discovered a serene space where anxious thoughts could not intrude. Tai Chi taught me that strength lies in softness, and resilience in flow."

Alex's journey with Tai Chi unfolds as a dance of peace, illustrating the transformative impact of this ancient practice on mental well-being. The rhythmic flow of Tai Chi provided Alex with a serene space, free from the intrusion of anxious thoughts. Through the practice of Tai Chi, he embraced the philosophy that strength can be found in softness and resilience in the graceful flow of movements.

Embracing the Serenity Within:

As we immerse ourselves in the practices of Yoga and Tai Chi, let us embrace the serenity that unfolds within each intentional breath and mindful movement. These ancient arts become not only tools for anxiety management but gateways to a harmonious union of body and mind. The interplay of breath, movement, and mindfulness transcends the boundaries of traditional exercise, offering a holistic approach to well-being.

The essence of yoga and Tai Chi lies in their ability to create a sanctuary within, where individuals can find solace, balance, and resilience. The intentional exploration of breath and movement becomes a transformative journey, fostering a profound connection with the present moment. In the upcoming sections, we will continue our exploration of alternative therapies, each offering a unique tapestry of well-being for those seeking holistic approaches to anxiety management.

The Power of Community and Group Support

In the intricate tapestry of anxiety management, the threads of community and group support weave a resilient fabric of understanding, shared experiences, and profound healing. This section invites you to explore the therapeutic power inherent in connecting with others who traverse similar paths, finding solace, strength, and camaraderie in the embrace of a supportive community.

Unveiling the Therapeutic Tapestry:

Community as a Pillar of Support:

Discover how the sense of belonging to a community or support group can be a transformative force in the journey of anxiety management. Explore the shared challenges, victories, and collective wisdom that emerge when individuals with similar experiences come together in a supportive environment.

In the intricate landscape of anxiety, the role of community becomes a vital pillar of support. When individuals facing similar challenges unite, a powerful therapeutic tapestry is woven. This shared journey fosters a sense of understanding that extends beyond words, creating a space where victories are celebrated collectively, challenges are faced together, and collective wisdom becomes a guiding light.

Navigating Isolation through Connection:

Anxiety can breed feelings of isolation, but within the community, individuals find a refuge. Uncover the significance of shared understanding, empathetic listening, and the knowledge that you are not alone in your struggles. The collective strength of a community becomes a beacon in the darkest moments.

In the solitude that anxiety often brings, the warmth of a supportive community acts as a balm. The understanding hearts, empathetic ears, and shared experiences create a refuge against the isolating nature of anxiety. The power of connection within a community serves as a lifeline, offering solace and strength to individuals navigating their unique paths.

Joining Support Groups:

Finding Your Tribe:

Embark on a journey to discover and join support groups tailored to your specific needs. Whether in-person or online, support groups offer a sanctuary where individuals can share, learn, and grow together. Gain insights into the different types of groups available, from those focused on specific anxiety disorders to general well-being.

Finding the right support group is akin to discovering a tribe that understands your language without words. This journey involves exploring various avenues, from local in-person groups to online communities. Each support group becomes a unique space where individuals find resonance, understanding, and a shared commitment to well-being.

Tips for Effective Participation:

Delve into practical advice on how to actively engage and benefit from a support group. From the importance of open communication to the role of active listening, this section provides guidance for creating a meaningful and supportive experience within a group setting.

Participation in a support group is not merely about attendance but active engagement. Practical tips for effective participation include fostering open communication, practicing active listening, and embracing the diversity of experiences within the group. These guidelines create an environment where every voice is heard, and collective wisdom becomes a powerful force.

Stories of Camaraderie and Support:

Maria's Healing Circle:

"In our support group, I found a circle of understanding hearts. Sharing my journey with anxiety felt like lifting a weight off my shoulders. We celebrated victories, comforted each other during setbacks, and, most importantly, reminded one another that we were never alone."

Maria's narrative epitomizes the healing circle that a support group forms. The understanding hearts within the community create a safe space for vulnerability and shared experiences. Through celebrations and comforting moments, the group becomes a source of strength, emphasizing the interconnectedness that dispels the sense of isolation.

Tom's Online Tribe:

"Living in a small town, finding a local support group was challenging. Joining an online community opened up a world of support. The virtual connections I made became a lifeline, proving that the power of community transcends geographical boundaries."

Tom's story reflects the transformative reach of online communities. Despite geographical limitations, the online tribe becomes a lifeline, emphasizing that the power of community transcends physical boundaries. Virtual connections foster a sense of belonging and support, proving that community knows no borders.

Embracing the Healing Collective:

As we navigate the expansive landscape of alternative and complementary therapies, let us recognize the profound healing that unfolds within the embrace of community and group support. In the upcoming sections, we will continue our exploration, each chapter offering a diverse avenue for those seeking holistic approaches to anxiety management.

The healing collective formed by communities and support groups becomes a testament to the strength found in unity. As individuals share their stories, insights, and collective wisdom, the therapeutic tapestry expands, offering solace and empowerment. Embracing the healing collective becomes a pivotal step in the holistic journey toward well-being, reinforcing that the support of others is a powerful force in the face of anxiety's challenges. In the chapters ahead, we will continue to unravel various threads of alternative therapies, each contributing to the diverse and comprehensive guide for anxiety management.

Chapter 8: Celebrating Progress

In the intricate tapestry of anxiety management, the journey toward a new life free from anxiety is marked by milestones, courage, and transformative growth. This chapter invites you to reflect on the progress made, acknowledging the steps taken towards a brighter, more resilient future. Let us explore the art of celebrating progress, an essential practice that illuminates the path to a life unburdened by anxiety.

Embracing Milestones

The Significance of Acknowledgment:

Recognizing progress is a powerful act of self-affirmation. Dive into the importance of acknowledging the small victories and milestones along the way. Each step forward, no matter how seemingly insignificant, contributes to the tapestry of personal growth and resilience.

In the journey of anxiety management, acknowledgment becomes a cornerstone. By acknowledging the significance of small victories, individuals affirm their progress and resilience. The act of recognizing each step forward, regardless of its scale, plays a pivotal role in weaving the fabric of personal growth.

Reflecting on the Journey:

Encourage readers to take moments of reflection, revisiting the early stages of their anxiety management journey. By recognizing the distance traveled and the lessons learned, individuals gain a deeper appreciation for their evolving selves.

Reflection becomes a compass guiding individuals through their anxiety management journey. By revisiting the early stages, one gains insight into the transformative process, acknowledging the resilience and wisdom acquired along the way. It is through reflection that the journey's significance becomes more profound.

Ideas for Acknowledging Progress:

Personal Progress Journal:

Suggest the creation of a personal progress journal where readers can document their achievements, no matter how small. This tangible record becomes a testament to resilience, serving as a source of motivation during challenging times.

Encourage the practice of documenting progress in a personal journal. Each entry, capturing achievements and triumphs, becomes a tangible testament to resilience. The journal serves as a source of inspiration, offering motivation during moments of challenge and doubt.

Celebratory Rituals:

Explore the concept of creating celebratory rituals around milestones. From a quiet moment of self-reflection to a shared celebration with loved ones, these rituals infuse the journey with a sense of accomplishment and joy.

Introduce the idea of incorporating celebratory rituals into the journey. Whether through moments of quiet self-reflection or shared celebrations with loved ones, these rituals become symbolic expressions of accomplishment and joy. They contribute to shaping a positive and rewarding narrative.

Inspiring Stories of Triumph:

Sophia's Journey to Liberation:

"For years, anxiety held me captive. Each step forward felt like an uphill battle. Celebrating my progress, no matter how modest, became my compass. It was in those celebrations that I discovered the strength to continue, and eventually, the courage to live free from anxiety."

Sophia's narrative exemplifies the transformative power of celebrating progress. In the face of anxiety's captivity, each acknowledgment became a guiding compass. The celebrations, no matter how modest, were the stepping stones toward the courage to live a life free from anxiety.

James's Triumph Over Fear:

"Anxiety whispered doubt into every decision I made. Acknowledging my progress was a game-changer. I started facing fears I never thought I could conquer. Today, anxiety is no longer the director of my life, and each celebration is a victory dance."

James's story portrays the profound impact of acknowledging progress in overcoming anxiety. The act of recognition empowered him to confront doubts and conquer fears thought insurmountable. Today, anxiety no longer dictates his life, and every celebration becomes a joyous victory dance.

Embracing the Journey:

As we navigate the final chapters of this transformative guide, let us embrace the spirit of celebrating progress. Each acknowledgement, every milestone celebrated, becomes a brushstroke in the canvas of a new life—one free from the shackles of anxiety. In the upcoming sections, we will continue our exploration, delving into avenues that empower individuals to shape their narratives and live with newfound freedom.

Maintaining Progress

Strategies for Nurturing Progress:

Reflecting on Resilience:

Encourage readers to reflect on the resilience they've cultivated throughout their anxiety management journey. Acknowledge that setbacks may occur, but true strength is found in recognizing one's ability to bounce back.

In the journey towards anxiety management, fostering resilience becomes a cornerstone. Encourage readers to reflect on the resilience they have cultivated, emphasizing that setbacks are part of the process. True strength lies in the ability to recognize and rebound from these challenges.

Mindfulness as a Daily Practice:

Highlight the role of mindfulness as a daily practice in nurturing progress. Through mindfulness, individuals cultivate awareness of their thoughts and emotions, creating a foundation for intentional living and sustained well-being.

In nurturing progress, emphasize the significance of mindfulness as a daily practice. Through mindfulness, individuals develop an acute awareness of their thoughts and emotions, laying the groundwork for intentional living and enduring well-being.

Building a Support Network:

Discuss the importance of maintaining a robust support network. Whether through friends, family, or support groups, having a circle of understanding individuals contributes to ongoing emotional support and accountability.

Explore the vital role of a strong support network in nurturing progress. Whether it involves friends, family, or support groups, emphasize the value of a community that provides ongoing emotional support and accountability.

Checklist for Daily Practices:

Mindful Breathing Exercises:

Include mindful breathing exercises in the daily routine. Short moments of intentional breathing serve as anchors, fostering a sense of calm and grounding in the face of stressors.

Incorporate mindful breathing exercises into the daily routine. These brief moments of intentional breathing act as anchors, instilling a sense of calm and grounding, especially in the face of stressors.

Reflection and Gratitude:

Encourage individuals to incorporate reflection and gratitude into their daily rituals. Taking stock of positive experiences and expressing gratitude helps maintain a positive mindset and reinforces a sense of progress.

Inspire individuals to integrate reflection and gratitude into their daily rituals. The practice of acknowledging positive experiences and expressing gratitude becomes a cornerstone for maintaining a positive mindset and reinforcing progress.

Self-Compassion Practices:

Emphasize self-compassion as an essential daily practice. Encourage readers to be gentle with themselves, especially during challenging moments, fostering a nurturing inner dialogue.

Highlight self-compassion as a fundamental daily practice. Urge readers to embrace self-kindness, particularly during challenging moments, cultivating a nurturing inner dialogue.

Examples of Vigilance and Maintenance:

Lisa's Daily Mindfulness Routine:

"Each morning, I dedicate a few minutes to mindfulness. It sets a positive tone for my day. Even when life gets hectic, this simple practice keeps me grounded, preventing old anxieties from resurfacing."

Incorporate Lisa's daily mindfulness routine as an exemplary practice. Her dedication to a few minutes of mindfulness each morning, setting a positive tone, becomes a valuable model for preventing the resurgence of old anxieties during life's hectic moments.

Tom's Support System Check-In:

"I've made it a habit to connect with someone from my support system every day. It's a quick check-in where we share our highs and lows. This daily practice not only strengthens our bond but acts as a protective shield against anxiety's return."

Showcase Tom's support system check-in as a commendable practice. His habit of daily connections with someone from his support system, sharing highs and lows, exemplifies a ritual that not only strengthens bonds but acts as a protective shield against the return of anxiety.

Embracing Sustained Well-Being:

As we delve into the strategies for nurturing progress, remember that the journey doesn't end—it transforms. By seamlessly integrating these practices into daily life, individuals pave the way for a sustained sense of well-being. In the subsequent sections, we will explore additional facets of embracing a new life free from anxiety, empowering readers to chart their course toward lasting resilience and joy.

Live a Life of Fullness

Inspiring a Life of Fulfillment:

Redrawing Life's Canvas:

Encourage readers to view this phase not as an endpoint but as a vibrant beginning. With the tools acquired on their anxiety management journey, they now possess the palette to redraw life's canvas with vibrant hues of joy, purpose, and fulfillment.

Encourage readers to embrace this phase not as a conclusion but as an exhilarating commencement. Armed with the tools garnered on their anxiety management journey, they now wield the palette to paint life's canvas with vibrant hues of joy, purpose, and fulfillment.

Setting New Goals:

Guide individuals in setting new goals that extend beyond anxiety management. Whether it's pursuing a passion, embracing a new hobby, or charting a career path, these goals become beacons illuminating the path to a fulfilling life.

Guide individuals in formulating goals that surpass the realm of anxiety management. Whether it involves pursuing a passion, embracing a new hobby, or charting a career path, these goals become beacons that illuminate the path to a life of fulfillment.

Embracing New Opportunities:

Explore the concept of seizing new opportunities that align with their authentic selves. This might involve stepping out of comfort zones, taking on challenges, or embarking on adventures that resonate with their newfound sense of resilience.

Explore the concept of seizing fresh opportunities that align with their authentic selves. This might involve stepping out of comfort zones, taking on challenges, or embarking on adventures that resonate with their newfound sense of resilience.

Guidance for Living Fully:

Cultivating Mindfulness in Daily Life:

Emphasize the integration of mindfulness into daily life. Living fully involves being present in each moment, savoring experiences, and cultivating gratitude for the richness that life offers.

Emphasize the integration of mindfulness into daily life. Living fully involves being present in each moment, savoring experiences, and cultivating gratitude for the richness that life offers.

Fostering Healthy Relationships:

Highlight the importance of fostering healthy and meaningful connections. Encourage readers to surround themselves with individuals who uplift, inspire, and contribute positively to their journey.

Highlight the importance of nurturing healthy and meaningful connections. Encourage readers to surround themselves with individuals who uplift, inspire, and contribute positively to their journey.

Balancing Work and Leisure:

Discuss the significance of balancing work and leisure. Living fully entails not only pursuing career ambitions but also allocating time for relaxation, recreation, and the pursuit of passions.

Discuss the significance of balancing work and leisure. Living fully entails not only pursuing career ambitions but also allocating time for relaxation, recreation, and the pursuit of passions.

Motivational Stories:

Emma's Blossoming Career:

"After conquering my anxiety, I redirected my energy into a career that truly fulfills me. Every day is an opportunity to contribute to something meaningful, and I've discovered a sense of purpose that goes beyond managing anxiety."

"After overcoming anxiety, I redirected my energy into a career that truly fulfills me. Every day presents an opportunity to contribute to something meaningful, and I've discovered a sense of purpose that extends beyond managing anxiety."

Alex's Adventure Across Continents:

"Anxiety used to confine me, but now I embrace the unknown. I've traveled to places I once only dreamed of, and in each journey, I've found liberation from the constraints of fear. Life post-anxiety is an extraordinary adventure."

"Anxiety used to confine me, but now I embrace the unknown. I've traveled to places I once only dreamed of, and in each journey, I've found liberation from the constraints of fear. Life post-anxiety is an extraordinary adventure."

Embracing a Vibrant Life Beyond Anxiety:

As we navigate the terrain of living fully, remember that the journey is an ongoing evolution. By setting new goals, embracing opportunities, and nurturing a holistic approach to life, individuals step into a vibrant existence that transcends the confines of anxiety. In the following chapters, we will further explore the multifaceted aspects of this newfound life, empowering readers to savor the richness that awaits them.

Understanding the Therapeutic Essence of Giving

We've unraveled the reciprocity of healing inherent in the act of giving. It is not merely a selfless gesture but a therapeutic journey where the threads of our support weave seamlessly with the fabric of our recovery. By extending compassion to others, we find solace, purpose, and a sense of interconnectedness, reinforcing the foundation of our own well-being.

Building Empathy and Connection:

Our journey towards a life free from anxiety has been marked by a deepening sense of empathy and connection. Acts of kindness have not only illuminated the path but have become integral to the cornerstone of our newfound existence. As we extend a helping hand, we foster a profound sense of belonging and shared humanity, transcending the shadows of anxiety.

Suggestions for Volunteer Work and Community Involvement:

As we embrace this chapter, let us consider tangible ways to give back within our communities. Engaging in local initiatives, participating in neighborhood projects, or contributing to mental health advocacy are potent avenues. By involving ourselves in support groups and helplines, we create a ripple effect of support, providing guidance and comfort to those navigating the very journey we once walked.

Stories of Enriched Lives and Mitigated Anxiety:

The narratives of individuals who have walked this path before us echo with the resonance of enriched lives and mitigated anxiety. Sarah's journey as a peer mentor stands testament to the transformative power of sharing our stories. Her act of giving back became a lifeline, reinforcing her own recovery and fostering a profound sense of purpose.

David's volunteer work at a crisis helpline illuminates the profound fulfillment derived from connecting with others in their moments of vulnerability. Through these stories, we glimpse into the ongoing cycle of giving and recovery—an endless dance where the gifts we offer to others become profound gifts to ourselves.

Embracing the Fullness of Life:

As we conclude this transformative guide, let us remember that the journey doesn't end here; instead, it unfolds into the vibrant tapestry of a life free from anxiety. By embracing the fullness of life, setting new goals, nurturing healthy relationships, and continuing the cycle of giving, we become active participants in our well-being.

A Journey Unbounded

As we stand on the precipice of this final chapter, let the resonance of these words echo through the corridors of your being: the journey of anxiety management is not a conclusion but a perpetual exploration—a journey that continues to unfold with each step you take.

Anxiety, much like life itself, is dynamic—an ever-shifting landscape that demands our adaptability and resilience. Recognize that the path isn't a straight line; it meanders through peaks and valleys. In these undulations, you discover the essence of growth, refining your strategies as you deepen your understanding of yourself and your triggers.

Parting Words of Encouragement and Wisdom:

As you stand at this juncture, take a moment to reflect on the milestones you've crossed. Celebrate not only the grand victories but the quiet triumphs too. Each step, no matter how seemingly small, is a testament to your courage in facing anxiety head-on. Setbacks are not failures; they are invitations to learn, adapt, and grow.

In the face of anxiety, be gentle with yourself. Extend the same kindness and patience to yourself that you would to a dear friend. Your journey has been a testament to your resilience, a narrative of strength, and a commitment to a life unburdened by anxiety.

Resources for Continued Learning and Support:

But this is not a farewell; it's an invitation to a lifelong pursuit of well-being. To fuel your ongoing growth, consider the plethora of resources awaiting your exploration:

> Recommended Readings: Immerse yourself in books on anxiety management, mindfulness, and personal development. Let the written word be a guide, offering fresh perspectives and deepening your understanding of the intricate mind-body connection.

> Online Communities: Traverse the digital landscape and engage with supportive online communities. Share your experiences, absorb the wisdom of others, and revel in the camaraderie that blossoms when shared journeys intersect.

> Professional Support: Should the need arise, continue seeking guidance from mental health professionals. Therapy sessions, like beacons, provide ongoing support, assisting you in navigating challenges as they arise.

> Mindfulness and Meditation Apps: Infuse mindfulness into your daily routine through apps that offer guided sessions. These practices, like gentle currents, contribute to the reservoir of emotional resilience, fostering long-term well-being.

In parting, remember that you are equipped with the strength and tools to tread the path that stretches ahead. This chapter isn't the finale; it's a continuation—an inauguration into a life emancipated from anxiety, brimming with possibilities, growth, and a profound connection to your inner self. May your journey unfold with the grace of continued self-discovery, empowerment, and the fulfillment of a life guided by resilience and purpose. The canvas is yours to paint, and the brush is in your hands.

Conclusion: Embracing a Life Beyond Anxiety

Within these pages, you've embarked on a profound journey—a quest of self-discovery, resilience, and empowerment. As we conclude this transformative exploration, let's reflect on the key teachings that have paved the way for a life free from the constraints of anxiety.

Summarizing the Essential Lessons:

Throughout this book, we've delved into the intricate landscape of anxiety, unraveling its threads and discovering powerful tools for managing its grip. From the early chapters, where we identified and named our emotions, to the strategies for coping with intense emotional experiences, each section has been a stepping stone toward greater emotional well-being.

The art of self-compassion has been a guiding light, fostering a compassionate dialogue with oneself amidst the challenges of anxiety. We've explored the profound impact of healthy emotional expression and communication, recognizing the therapeutic power of community and support.

Reaffirming the Message of Hope:

As we stand on the precipice of a new chapter, let the resounding message be one of hope. Your journey doesn't end here; it transforms into a life rich with possibilities. Engaging in this exploration signifies your courage and commitment to a life beyond anxiety.

Hope is not just a sentiment; it's a powerful force that propels us forward. You've learned that managing anxiety is not about eradicating emotions but about befriending them, navigating their ebbs and flows with resilience and self-compassion.

The Call to Action: Living the Principles:

Now, armed with knowledge and tools, the call to action is clear. It's about living the principles you've discovered—continuing practices that resonate with you, adapting them to the ever-changing landscape of your life, and embracing the ongoing journey of self-discovery.

> Practice Mindfulness Daily: Incorporate mindfulness into your daily routine, whether through meditation, mindful breathing, or simply being present in each moment. It's a practice that nourishes the soul and fosters emotional resilience.

> Express Yourself Authentically: Continue to express your emotions healthily, recognizing the power of open communication. Share your thoughts and fears with trusted loved ones and nurture connections that provide support.

> Cultivate Self-Compassion: Be your own ally. In moments of challenge, extend the same kindness to yourself that you would offer a friend. Your relationship with yourself is the cornerstone of resilience.

Explore Additional Resources: The journey of self-discovery is vast. Continue exploring books, articles, and online communities that align with your growth. Seek professional support if needed, for there is strength in reaching out.

Embracing a Life Beyond Anxiety:

As you move forward, may you carry with you the wisdom gained from these pages. Embrace uncertainties with courage and savor joys with gratitude. Your journey doesn't end here; it's a continuum—an ever-unfolding narrative where you, the author of your story, navigate a life free from the constraints of anxiety.

In closing, let these final words resonate: You are resilient. You are worthy. You have the power to shape the narrative of your life. With hope as your guide, step into the realm of possibility. This is your journey—embrace it fully, and may it be a testament to the strength within you.